Did You Miss the Rapture?

A Study of Dispensational Premillennialism

Mack Lyon

Publishing Designs, Inc.
Huntsville, Alabama

Publishing Designs, Inc.
P. O. Box 3241
Huntsville, Alabama 35810

© 1993 by Mack Lyon

All rights reserved. No part of this book may be reproduced or transmitted without written permission from Publishing Designs, Inc., except for the inclusion of short quotations in a review.

Fourth Printing, 2001

Cover design by Gary Pollock

Printed in the United States of America

ISBN 0-929540-15-8

To the elders of the
Edmond, Oklahoma Church of Christ
who have faithfully and generously
supported me in the television ministry
for more than a decade,
and who have encouraged me always
to speak the truth in love.

Editor's Preface

The material presented in *Did You Miss the Rapture?* was developed for television and delivered by its author in the late 1980s and early 1990s. The speaker's script was so refined and exact that almost no editing was required. However, those procedures necessary for transferring spoken messages to the printed page so they can best be understood by the reader are set forth here for the careful student.

Though current events presented herein have already slipped into the pages of history, expressions such as "a few days ago," "Saddam Hussein," and "Desert Storm" have been left intact. They give spontaneity to the messages and will spark the interest of thousands of readers for many years to come.

Pronouns having reference to deity and not quoted from other sources are capitalized: He, His, Him, and Himself.

All quoted materials, including archaic spellings, are produced as in their original text with the following exceptions:

(1) Capital letters that begin Bible verses have been changed to lowercase when they do not begin sentences or begin complete statements that would normally be enclosed in quotation marks.

(2) Words or phrases emphasized by the author are italicized without any further indication that the emphases are his.

(3) Author's comments, when interspersed with quoted material, are set off in brackets with no further explanation.

With great joy and much enthusiasm, we place this book in the hands of curious seekers and sincere students of God's word. May God's blessings rest with the earnest reader!

James B. Andrews

Preface

Dispensational premillennialism has spread so rapidly in recent years that it is now the predominate view in most every denomination. While it may not be the "official" teaching of some of the mainline churches, it is the view held by virtually all the members and a vast majority of the younger pastors. The televangelists, self-styled prophets, and many others have been persistent in their propagation of the doctrine, while others of us have not said much out in the open.

We did address those erroneous teachings in our television program, *In Search of the Lord's Way*, and the messages contained in this volume are transcripts of those sermons. They have been edited only to eliminate credits, mail offerings, and the like. They were not delivered in series nor in the sequence in which they appear here. They are not exhaustive; there is much more to be said on every subject than is possible to say in a twelve-to-fifteen minute sermon. Some of the subjects have been repeated in other programs to comply with the need to say more.

These programs drew some of the heaviest mail response and telephone requests for copies of any programs we have ever done, which is indicative of the need and interest in the truth on these subjects. Many viewers suggested publishing them in a book so the material covered in those programs might be available in one volume.

The idea for thirteen chapters with questions for class discussion came from the number of requests received from churches, many denominations, for videos of those programs for use in Bible classes. The book goes forth with the prayer that it will not only be helpful to people who are searching for Bible answers to the questions raised by dispensational premillennial teaching that fills the current media, but also to churches in providing positive teaching on these things in their Bible classes.

I cannot claim originality to all the material presented here. Had I planned the material for publication in book form as I researched each subject, I certainly would have made notes on sources such as commentaries, magazine articles, and books. Now, after the passing of time, try as I have to identify sources, I cannot. I pray those authors who may recognize some of their original material here will write me, and in the next printing, we will gladly give due credit.

I owe much thanks to a lot of people: to the many who insisted on the publication of the material, to my friend Phil Sanders for his assistance with some of it, and to Dr. William E. Jones of the Oklahoma Christian University of Science and Arts Bible faculty for his help, especially in understanding Revelation. I am grateful, too, to my efficient secretary Shani for editing and preparing the material for publication.

But I am especially thankful to our Lord Jesus Christ who has counted me faithful, putting me into the ministry of His word and enabling me to reach so many people with the message of salvation in His name.

Mack Lyon

Contents

1. Premillennialism 1
2. The Gospel of the Kingdom 9
3. Did You Miss the Rapture? 17
4. Armageddon, the End of Time? 25
5. Daniel 2 and the Kingdom of Christ 33
6. Israel and the Land Promise 41
7. Antichrist and the Mark of the Beast 49
8. Revelations and Coming Events 57
9. Understanding Revelation 65
10. Matthew 24 73
11. The Second Coming of Christ 81
12. The Thousand Years of Revelation 20 89
13. The Hope a Christian Has 97

1

Premillennialism

I Corinthians 15:22-26

For as in Adam all die, even so in Christ shall all be made alive. But every man in his own order: Christ the firstfruits; afterward they that are Christ's at his coming. Then cometh the end, when he shall have delivered up the kingdom to God, even the Father; when he shall have put down all rule and all authority and power. For he must reign, till he hath put all enemies under his feet. The last enemy that shall be destroyed is death.

An advertisement in a popular magazine claims:

> Crime and corruption are rampant in the world and, according to the Bible, retribution comes as a consequence. The world is suffering a great "time of trouble." There is much cause of great rejoicing, however, because this dark cloud of trouble has a silver lining. God's new invisible and visible supernatural government will soon be established on earth, and will make it a worldwide paradise. Crime and corruption will be abolished, and all men of goodwill can then have everlasting safety, peace, joy, and life. For details write . . .

And then the address is given.

What does the Bible really say about the universal reign or kingdom of Christ? Are current events in the Middle East signs of His near return to establish a reign of peace here on the earth?

These things are the elements of the body of doctrine called *premillennialism*. This is a big word we seldom hear in sermons, yet we hear a lot of preaching about it. *Pre* means "before" and *millennium* has to do with a "thousand," so we are talking about something that is before a thousand. As it relates to religion, it is the theology or the doctrine of the return of Christ *before* His thousand year reign.

There are also people who are called *post-millennialists*, because of their belief that there is yet a golden age of righteousness and peace for the church at the end of which is Christ's return and the resurrection. There are also *amillennialists* who do not believe the Bible teaches such a millennium.

However, what we are hearing today is not pure premillennialism. It is a mixture of premillennialism with dispensationalism which holds to the idea that God created the world in six days and rested on the seventh. And because Peter said that with the Lord one day is as a thousand years and a thousand years are as one day (II Peter 3:8), all of human history is divided into seven dispensations. And since God rested on the seventh day, the return of Christ will be somewhere near the end of this century or the beginning of the next millennium.

When you combine these, you have many of the ideas being preached so much on television and radio, seen in the religious press, and heard discussed in much religious conversation. We cannot examine every detail of these teachings, but let us quickly overview them.

First is the idea that Jesus Christ came into the world at the time of His incarnation to establish His kingdom, His universal reign among men; but the divine plan was thwarted by His unexpected rejection by the Jews and His crucifixion. However, Jesus, foreseeing that event, rather than suffer total defeat, established the church instead as sort of an afterthought or interim arrangement. Then He is supposed to have promised He would come again at which time He would establish the kingdom as originally planned which He could not establish the first time.

He is said to have given a number of signs of His return, many of which are supposedly recorded in Matthew 24. It is taught that when He returns, He will come *very quietly*. Many people will not even know about it. He will snatch the saints away in some sort of a "rapture," but life will go on for the others: the people left on the earth, the wicked and the unconverted of course. The "raptured" will be with the Lord somewhere for a period of seven years.

Meanwhile back on the earth there will be a seven-year period of great tribulation—such tribulation as the world has never experienced. During the first three and one-half years of the tribulation period, the Jews will all be returned to Palestine and there will be a restoration of their religion. They will rebuild the temple which Solomon built and revive the system of animal sacrifices of the Law of Moses of the Old Testament period.

The second half of that seven-year period is supposed to be characterized by a great conflict, a terribly disastrous war which is called the battle of Armageddon. That conflict is to end with the third coming of Christ, this time *with* His saints, when He will establish His throne in Jerusalem and rule the world in a universal reign of peace and plenty for a thousand years. At the end of the thousand years, He is supposed to deliver up the kingdom to God; there will be judgment and, following the judgment, eternity.

Now these are the basic and fundamental elements of dispensational premillennialism. Of course, mixed in with all of this are the ideas of an antichrist and a lot of other dressings which we will discuss in other lessons. I hasten to say that the general theory which we have outlined very briefly may not suitably describe in detail the theory you have been hearing—or teaching. It would be impossible, even if we were disposed to do it, to detail every modern prophet's private speculation or supposed revelation directly from God. We have only intended to present a general overview.

There is no doubt that most premillennialists are sincere people, but there are some things I question about the basic tenets of their theology. I am sure you, too, want to know what the Bible really teaches about these matters. We will search the Scriptures and you will see it does make a difference.

First, to say that it was a part of the divine plan for Christ to establish His kingdom when He came into the world by the virgin Mary, but that He was defeated in that purpose by the unexpected rejection of the Jews and crucifixion, is to deny the sovereign will and power of God! My friend, God was not defeated when the Jews rejected His Son. His plan was not overthrown at the cross. Neither was the crucifixion unforeseen or unanticipated by Him. The Holy Spirit says:

> Forasmuch as ye know that ye were not redeemed with corruptible things, as silver and gold, from your vain conversation received by tradition from your fathers; but with the precious blood of Christ, as of a lamb without blemish and without spot: who verily was *foreordained before the foundation of the world*, but was manifest in these last times for you (I Peter 1:18-20).

Less than two months after the crucifixion, Peter preached to the Jews who had done it:

> Ye men of Israel, hear these words; Jesus of Nazareth, a man approved of God among you by miracles and wonders and signs, which God did by him in the midst of you, as ye yourselves also know: him, being delivered by the determinate counsel and foreknowledge of God, ye have taken, and by wicked hands have crucified and slain (Acts 2:22, 23).

Jesus' death for our sins was *foreknown* and *predetermined* of God unto our salvation. To hold, then, that it came as a surprise to Him and He was forced to alter His plan for the Messiah is tantamount to a denial of God's infinite will and unlimited power and a repudiation of His scheme of redemption by way of the cross.

Later, on the occasion of the healing of a lame man at the Beautiful gate of the temple, Peter spoke to some of these same people again about the death of Christ and said:

> And now, brethren I wot [know] that through ignorance ye did it, as did also your rulers. But those things which God before had shewed, by the mouth of all his prophets, that Christ should suffer, he hath so fulfilled (Acts 3:17, 18).

So, rather than being an historical accident, the rejection of the Messiah, resulting in His death, was actually a fulfillment of, not only God's *purpose*, but also His *prophecies*. He had foretold it! It had occurred just as He had planned it and as the prophets had said.

Then there is the matter of His establishing the church as an afterthought, an interim arrangement. My friend, this cannot be true because, with reference to his ministry to the Gentiles, Paul said it was:

> To make all men see what is the fellowship of the mystery, which from the beginning of the world hath been hid in God, who created all things by Jesus Christ: to the intent that now unto the principalities and powers in heavenly places might be known by *the church* the manifold wisdom of God, *according to the eternal purpose which he purposed* in Christ Jesus our Lord (Ephesians 3:9-12).

So the church is not an afterthought; not a substitute; not an ad-lib, thrown-together, provisional arrangement; but a vital part of God's purpose in Christ from before the world began.

It is obvious to the careful reader of the first four books of the New Testament, the *Gospels* (Matthew, Mark, Luke, and John), that Jesus really believed He was the Messiah. He not only considered His mission as bringing individual salvation to the lost (Luke 19:10), but also to establish a reign over the community of those who receive that salvation and submit to

Him as their king (Matthew 16:13-19). The Messiah was to be a king, but there can be no king in the absence of people who submit to his kingship. So to deny Jesus His kingship is to deny Him His Messiahship. If there is no kingdom, there is no king; therefore, no Messiah.

The Old Testament prophets spoke and wrote for centuries that when the Messiah came, He would establish His kingdom. Premillennialists do not deny these prophecies. As a matter of fact, they preach a lot about them, but they deny that Christ fulfilled them at His first coming and apply them to some later appearance. We will discuss some of those prophecies in particular in other lessons. But for now, two things are important concerning "unfulfilled" prophecies.

First, Jesus said He fulfilled them. In Luke 24:44, after His resurrection, He said to the eleven apostles (Judas had betrayed Him and hanged himself):

> These are the words which I spake unto you, while I was yet with you, that all things must be fulfilled, which were written in the law of Moses, and in the prophets, and in the psalms, concerning me.

Jesus fulfilled *everything* Moses said in the law about Him, *everything* in the *Psalms,* and *everything* the Old Testament prophets had written concerning the Messiah.

The Jews knew their Scriptures well and if they could have produced just one scripture in the *Law,* the *Psalms,* or the *Prophets* concerning Him that He did not fulfill, they could have proven Him a liar, a deceiver, and an imposter; and Christianity would never have been born. One of the weightiest evidences we have of the deity of Jesus Christ is His fulfillment of every Old Testament Scripture about Him. Now, centuries later, some people are saying He did not actually *fulfill* the kingdom prophecies; He *postponed* them.

That brings us to the second thing we need to consider about prophecy. It is that the time element of prophecy is as critical as any other. If a prophecy did not come to pass when the prophet said it would, he was a false prophet. Deuteronomy 18:22 says:

> When a prophet speaketh in the name of the Lord, if the thing follow not, nor come to pass, that is the thing which the Lord hath not spoken, but the prophet hath spoken it presumptuously.

Do you get the idea? If the kingdom prophecies were not fulfilled as they were supposed to be at Christ's first coming, but postponed, that makes Daniel, Isaiah, and all the others false prophets.

I am sure you can see now that it is important to decide whether or not to believe the premillennial theology. It is critical to your acceptance or denial of other very basic teachings of the Bible. It seems that every time there is a new development in the Mid-east, modern prophets have a heyday with fantasies about how it all fits into some personal interpretation of prophecy about the sudden return of Christ and the end of the world.

You have only to glance at the church page of your newspaper to know what I am saying is true. So it is not surprising that we are hearing a lot about it right now. As you have surely noticed, these so-called seers are constantly having to revise their fabrications. The antichrist of yesteryear is not today's; the dates set a few weeks ago were "miscalculations" and have had to be revised, yet they are purported to be divinely inspired and delivered directly to the prophet. If we are not careful, it will be as Jesus taught—the blind will be leading the blind.

We are receiving a lot of questions about why we do not preach more from the book of Revelation and what the Bible teaches about these things. There is a need to address such matters, especially since they are of such general interest, but we do not run a constant harangue about them as some others do because there are other biblical themes that are important, too.

We hope you are a Christian and living the life to the very fullest. But if you are not, we feel the urgent need to exhort you to become a Christian at once. Every day you delay becoming a child of God, you deprive yourself of the love, joy, peace, and all of what it means to be in right relationship with God. Accept Christ, be immersed into Him, buried with Him in baptism, risen with Him by the power that raised Him from the dead to live the new life of the Christian (Romans 6:3, 4; Colossians 2:12). God bless you. I love you.

QUESTIONS FOR CLASS DISCUSSION

1. What is premillennialism? postmillennialism? amillennialism? Which do you believe?
2. What is dispensationalism?
3. Give a general overview of the dispensational premillennial theory.
4. What would you say about "unfulfilled prophecy"?
5. Discuss some Bible doctrines that are contradicted by dispensational premillennialism.
6. If you were preaching, would you spend more time than most preachers in churches of Christ do, preaching from the book of Revelation and prophecy? Why?

2

The Gospel of the Kingdom

Mark 1: 14, 15

Now after that John was put in prison, Jesus came into Galilee, preaching the gospel of the kingdom of God, and saying, The time is fulfilled, and the kingdom of God is at hand: repent ye, and believe the gospel.

In the long ago, one of God's great prophets admonished the people:

> Seek ye the Lord while he may be found, call ye upon him while he is near: let the wicked forsake his way, and the unrighteous man his thoughts: and let him return unto the Lord, and he will have mercy upon him: and to our God, for he will abundantly pardon. For my thoughts are not your thoughts, neither are your ways my ways, saith the Lord. For as the heavens are higher than the earth, so are my ways higher than your ways, and my thoughts than your thoughts (Isaiah 55:6-9).

Well, it must be obvious to most of us that we need a better way than the chaotic way we are pursuing now in which every one goes his (or her) own way and does his own thing. If we are really serious about a better life and a better society, we might try the Lord's way, don't you think?

Bible students know that the word *gospel* literally and simply means "good news, glad tidings, or a good message." And even though it seldom is, *gospel* could be used with reference to any kind of good news such as the national economy, the birth of a baby, pardon for a prisoner, a medical report, or a job promotion. We have reserved its use almost exclusively for religious purposes: gospel music, gospel meetings, gospel broadcasts, to name a few. And I do not know whether you have noticed, but we use it only with reference to the religion of Christ—not Buddhism, not Hinduism, not Islam, not even Judaism—only Christianity.

The word *gospel* appears 101 times in the King James Version of the New Testament. Christ's teachings are often spoken of simply as "the gospel," and in other places the word is followed by a prepositional phrase that gives it a special emphasis, such as Mark 1:14, 15:

> Now after that John was put in prison, Jesus came into Galilee, preaching the *gospel of the kingdom* of God, and saying, The time is fulfilled, and the kingdom of God is at hand: repent ye, and believe the gospel.

In spite of the fact that many theologians deny that Christ intended to build the church, it is obvious from His preaching that from the beginning He considered it to be a vital part of His earthly ministry. For centuries the Jewish prophets had foretold the coming of the Messiah who would establish the kingdom of God and reign over it as king. And when Jesus laid claim to being the Messiah, the establishment of a world community of believers over which He would reign became a necessity. To deny that was His intent and purpose, or to deny that He did it, would be to disclaim Him as the Messiah, the Son of God.

In our Scripture text, Mark declares this aspect of His ministry to be a crucial point of the gospel which He preached. He says, "After that John was put in prison, Jesus came into Galilee, preaching the gospel [good news] of the kingdom." Matthew indicates that right after His baptism and wilderness temptation in Judea, Jesus returned to Galilee where He went about "teaching in their synagogues, and preaching the gospel of the kingdom" (Matthew 4:23). Luke gives it the same treatment. He says, "He went throughout every city and village, preaching the glad tidings of the kingdom of God" (Luke 8:1). Then, the message of the kingdom is gospel—good news.

What did Jesus preach about the kingdom that made it such a glad message? We have already noted:

> Now after that John was put in prison, Jesus came into Galilee, preaching the gospel of the kingdom of God, and saying, The time is fulfilled, and the kingdom of God is at hand: repent ye, and believe the gospel (Mark 1:14, 15).

For centuries the Jews had been reading their Scriptures and anxiously looking forward to the coming of the Messiah who would establish the kingdom of God among them and rule over them forever. Now came Jesus saying, "The time is fulfilled." Can you imagine the excitement that kind of preaching generated? Their prophecies were going to be fulfilled before their very eyes! Generations of their foreparents had looked for, lived for, and even died for what they were going to be privileged to see and experience! God's plan for redemption was to occur in their very own generation! And to enforce His promise, He added, "The kingdom of God is at hand." The time is approaching!

On another occasion Jesus said to them, "I tell you of a truth." Now wait a minute, He says, "I'm telling you the truth." He always told the truth. He is the very embodiment of truth. He is truth incarnate. So why does He say, "I'm telling you the truth"? Because He wants to emphasize what He is about to say as clear, plain, unmistakable truth. He does not want us to miss it. He must have known there would be some who would be hard to convince. What is that truth? Here it is: "There be some standing here [not our twentieth century generation, but theirs, right there while He was speaking], which shall not taste of death, till they see the kingdom of God" (Luke 9:27). My friend, they were going to live to see the kingdom of God established. Did it happen?

Some say, "No, it didn't happen. Christ's plan was thwarted when the Jews crucified Him, and He postponed the establishment of His kingdom until His return—well, not the next time but the third time." They tell us that when He comes again, He will rapture the redeemed out of this world to rescue them from the great tribulation of seven years after which He will come again and establish His kingdom and reign for a thousand years.

But it is not so. Some of those people who heard Jesus preach did live to see the kingdom in existence and to be a part of it. The Holy Spirit said to the Christians at Colossae that God had delivered them from the power of darkness and translated them into the kingdom of His dear Son (Colossians 1:13). The writer of Hebrews said we have received a kingdom which cannot be shaken (or moved) (Hebrews 12:28); John, exiled on the lonely isle of Patmos, said he was in the kingdom (Revelation 1:9). That is good news for you and me, my friend, because when we become Christians, we too are delivered from the reign of darkness and translated into the kingdom of God's dear Son. Right now!

Many people who teach a future reign of Jesus in Jerusalem look to Revelation as proof. But every time the kingdom is mentioned in Revelation, it is mentioned as presently in existence. For example, Revelation 1:4-6 (American Standard Version) says, "John to the seven churches that are in Asia . . . Unto him that loveth us, and loosed us from our sins by his blood, and he made us to be a kingdom, to be priests unto his God." Just as surely as Christians are *now* priests—a royal priesthood (I Peter 2:9), the church is *presently* the kingdom of Christ. The same is true of Revelation 5:9, 10. Revelation 11:15 and 12:10 show the triumph of the kingdom of God over the kingdoms of the world because of the blood of the Lamb and the testimony of Christ pointing back to the cross and the resurrection of Christ at which time all authority was given to Him in heaven and on earth (Matthew 28:18; Acts 2:33-36). Christ *is* (present tense) "King of kings and Lord of lords"

The Gospel of the Kingdom 13

(Revelation 17:14; 19:16). So one reason the gospel is called the good news of the kingdom is because it is a reality—not a dream, a fantasy, or even a promise of God for future generations, but for us! Another good thing about the kingdom of God is that it is not a physical, political entity bounded by seas and rivers and mountain ranges; it is a spiritual kingdom, world-wide in its scope. Jesus told Pilate when he asked Him if He were the king of the Jews:

> My kingdom is not of this world: if my kingdom were of this world, then would my servants fight, that I should not be delivered to the Jews: but now is my kingdom not from hence (John 18:36).

In other words, if His kingdom were the kind the Jews (and multitudes today) expected it to be—a political, economic system with a police force and standing armies—Pilate would have had a fight on his hand. "My servants would fight," He said. But He assured Pilate that He was no challenge to Caesar in that regard.

What kind of a kingdom is it then? The Holy Spirit says, "The kingdom of God is not meat and drink; but righteousness, and peace, and joy in the Holy Spirit" (Romans 14:17). That is what it is all about then, righteousness! It is a kingdom of *righteousness* and *peace* and *joy*, not material possessions and world domination. If Jesus had come for that, He could have had it. The devil took Him up into a high mountain, showed Him all the kingdoms of the world and the glory of them, and said to Him, "All these things will I give thee, if thou wilt fall down and worship me" (Matthew 4:9). There is no doubt about it, he could have delivered.

Jesus knew there would always be people who would hunger and thirst after righteousness. In His kingdom, He said, they shall be filled because that is what it is all about (Matthew 5:6). Righteousness was originally spelled "rightwiseness" which expresses its real meaning—being wise to the right and just things in life. That is the kingdom of Christ. Without the influence of Christ's kingdom, this world would be uninhabitable. So the present existence of the kingdom of God is mighty good news today.

Another feature of the kingdom of Christ that is great news is that it cannot be shaken—it is an unmovable kingdom. A passage we mentioned in Hebrews says, "Wherefore we receiving a kingdom which cannot be moved, let us have grace, whereby we may serve God acceptably with reverence and godly fear" (Hebrews 12:28).

Nebuchadnezzar saw a vision of an image whose head was gold, his breast and his arms of silver, his belly and his thighs of brass, his legs of iron and his feet part of iron and part of clay. Daniel said these represent four (he specifically said four) consecutive world empires beginning with Babylon, followed by Persia, the Macedonians, and Rome. He said:

> In the days of these kings [that would be the Roman kings] shall the God of heaven set up a kingdom, which shall never be destroyed: and the kingdom shall not be left to other people, but it shall break in pieces and consume all these kingdoms, and it shall stand for ever (Daniel 2:44).

To make sure there is no misunderstanding, the Holy Spirit pinpoints the time of it all in Luke 3:1 as the fifteenth year of the reign of the Roman Emperor Tiberius Caesar that John the Baptist came preaching "the kingdom of heaven is at hand." The angel promised Mary:

> Behold thou shalt conceive in thy womb, and bring forth a son, and shalt call his name Jesus. He shall be great, and shall be called the Son of the Highest: and the Lord God shall give unto him the throne of his father, David: and he shall reign over the house of Jacob for ever; and of his kingdom there shall be no end.

That is a familiar passage in Luke 1:31-33, isn't it?

Empires may rise and collapse, thrones may topple and fall, but the kingdom of Christ is *unshakable* and *unmovable*. It will not be here today and gone tomorrow. It *will* endure for ever. In a world of uncertainties, it is great to be a citizen of the unshakable kingdom.

There is still another bit of good news I want to share with you about the kingdom of Christ. When Jesus comes and the dead are raised, Christ will then deliver that kingdom up to the Father, and God will become all in all. No, He will not come to establish the kingdom here on earth but to take it away into heaven. After proving the resurrection of the dead in the early verses of I Corinthians 15, Paul confidently affirms:

> Now is Christ risen from the dead, and become the firstfruits of them that slept. For since by man came death, by man came also the resurrection of the dead. For as in Adam all die, even so in Christ shall all be made alive. But every man in his own order. Christ the firstfruits, afterward they that are Christ's at his coming. Then cometh the end [not seven years of tribulation followed by a thousand year reign], when he shall have delivered up the kingdom to God, even the Father (I Corinthians 15:20-24).

Indeed, the gospel of Jesus Christ is good news about the kingdom:

(1) It is a present reality.

(2) It is a reign of righteousness and peace and joy.

(3) It is a permanent thing; it will not be overthrown.

(4) It will be ushered into a state of even greater glory when Jesus comes.

My friend are you a citizen?

Nicodemus learned that citizenship in the kingdom of Christ is not by natural birth; a person must be born again of water and the Spirit to enter it (John 3:1-7). He must believe in Christ, not just give mental assent to His deity, but lovingly and obediently put his trust in Him by being baptized in water. And having thereby made a commitment to Jesus, follow Him all the days of his life—unto death.

When my family and I had been in Australia for several months, the Australian government gave us the opportunity to become citizens of that great commonwealth. We liked it there. We enjoyed the time we spent there and were blessed by it. But becoming an Australian citizen would mean giving up our American citizenship. It is impossible to claim allegiance to two governments at the same time. Since we were not willing to renounce our citizenship here, we were denied it there.

You know, there is a spiritual application of that. A person cannot be a citizen of the kingdom of Christ while still owing allegiance to the world—the kingdom and the rule of Satan. He must renounce his loyalty to Satan to have citizenship in heaven as Paul said of Christians in Philippians 3:20. But in this case it is abundantly worth repudiating fidelity to the old native world to be born again to take up residence in Christ's new and eternal kingdom. If you have not done that, would you do it today? If we may assist you, give us a call. God bless you. I love you.

QUESTIONS FOR CLASS DISCUSSION

1. Discuss the meaning and use of the word *gospel*.
2. Give four reasons why the message preached by Jesus about the kingdom was a gospel message.
3. Discuss Nebuchadnezzar's dream in Daniel 2, the image and what it meant.
4. If our Lord had not intended to establish the kingdom at His first coming, how could His message have been interpreted as "good news"?
5. In what other ways is the gospel good news?
6. Discuss Jesus' answer to Pilate and what it means.
7. Who was Nicodemus? How did he learn that citizenship in the kingdom was not by natural birth?

3

Did You Miss the Rapture?

II Peter 3:9, 10

The Lord is not slack concerning his promise, as some men count slackness; but is longsuffering to us-ward, not willing that any should perish, but that all should come to repentance. But the day of the Lord will come as a thief in the night; in the which the heavens shall pass away with a great noise, and the elements shall melt with fervent heat, the earth also and the works that are therein shall be burned up.

A few days ago we were all alerted to the imminence of "the rapture." A fellow by the name of Whisenant wrote a book in which he predicted that Jesus would return at 11:00 A.M. CDT, Tuesday, September thirteenth. However, later he said that he failed to reckon with the International Date Line, so he made an adjustment in his calculations and reset the time to 9:55 A.M. CDT, Wednesday, September fourteenth. But Jesus did not come then, so Whisenant moved the date to Thursday the fifteenth and, if not then, to Friday the sixteenth. He said there was no way it would not come to pass.

Well, it did not come to pass or else Whisenant was not ready to go with the redeemed to be with the Savior and, along with the rest of us, just missed the rapture himself, because he is still around. And according to *Christianity Today* magazine (October 21), he is still saying that the rapture will occur sometime in 1988. "The evidence is all over the place," he says, "that it is going to be in a few weeks anyway." It was reported in the media that his book sold more than three million copies and that many people believed in him and supported him. They even sold their possessions, quit their jobs, and gathered together in church buildings to await the appearance of Christ. But it did not happen.

What about such speculative preaching as that? Why is it that such obviously false prophets can get such a following and nation-wide attention? What can we know about the coming of Christ?

The second coming of Christ is as fundamental to the Christian's faith as His incarnation, His death for our sins, His burial in Joseph's new tomb, and His resurrection from the dead. Ever since His ascension into heaven as recorded in Acts 1:9, His disciples have anxiously and excitedly looked forward to the day of His return. And for good reason. We have His own promise of it. Being the Son of God and knowing that the time of His departure was at hand, He announced to His chosen few that the time had come. Their hearts were heavy and He knew that, so He tried to comfort them. He said:

> Let not your heart be troubled: ye believe in God, believe also in me. In my Father's house are many mansions: if it were not so, I would have told you. I go to prepare a place for you. And if I go and prepare a place for you, I will come again, and receive you unto myself; that where I am, there ye may be also (John 14:1-3).

Furthermore, while they watched, He was taken up:

> ... and a cloud received him out of their sight. And while they looked stedfastly toward heaven as he went up, behold, two men stood by them in white apparel [angelic beings they were]; which also said, Ye men of Galilee, why stand ye gazing up into heaven? this same Jesus, which is taken up from you into heaven, shall so come in like manner as ye have seen him go into heaven (Acts 1:9-11).

Did You Miss the Rapture? 19

From that moment throughout the book of Acts, the Epistles, and even in Revelation the Holy Spirit has promised over and over that He is coming again. The devout Christian really believes it and that conviction affects the way he looks at life, the kind of person he is, what he does and does not do.

Over the years there have been many who have set dates for it. It is a matter of historical record that a William G. Miller predicted that Jesus would come in 1843, but like Edgar Whisenant, when it did not happen, he figured again and said he had missed it a year, that Christ would come in 1844. His followers robed themselves in white sheets and climbed up in the trees to wait for Him. But He did not come.

Another fellow by the name of Charles T. Russell set the date for October 1914, but he too miscalculated and reset it in 1915. Some believe and teach that He did come in 1914, but He came quietly and invisibly and was witnessed only by the faithful of their small sect. That same cult revised its teaching and set October 1, 1975 as the day. When Christ did not come that day, many of their adherents were disillusioned and left the sect. Since the formation of the State of Israel in 1948, many others have predicted that the "rapture" will occur within the present generation. Among the more notables have been Hal Lindsey and Herbert W. Armstrong.

Each of them has his own theory but, generally speaking, the idea is that at His incarnation, Christ came to establish His kingdom on the earth but was defeated in that mission by unexpected rejection by the Jewish nation. But so as not to be completely defeated, He established the church as sort of a substitute, stop-gap arrangement and promised to return to set up the kingdom.

He is supposed to have given signs of His return, some of which are supposedly recorded in Matthew 24. When He does return, it is supposed that He will come *quietly* and waft His saints away in what is called the "rapture." Some will be working at their jobs on the assembly line, at their computer posts, plowing their fields, or cleaning house. Whatever they are doing, it will be quietly interrupted; they will just disappear. Loved ones, associates, friends will miss them and will not know where they have gone. But Jesus will have supposedly taken them out of this world to be with Him for a period of seven years. The dead saints will also be raptured. Some of the graves in the cemeteries will be opened and the bodies gone, but no one will know where or why. The wicked will remain here on the earth (or in the graves) for a period of seven years of great tribulation.

During the first three and one-half years of that tribulation, the Jews will be returned to Palestine where they will rebuild the temple of Solomon and revive the Old Testament system of animal sacrifices. The tribulation period will be consummated with a great and terrible war which will be fought on the battlefield of Armageddon. But Christ will come *again* (the third appearance) and He will bring the battle to an end. He will establish His kingdom and reign over all the earth from His throne in Jerusalem for one thousand years of peace and prosperity. Then will come the end of the world, the judgment, and eternity.

What a fantasy! In so limited a time, we have not given all the details nor all the different versions. It has been said many times by many people, and it is true, that religious confusion exists, not because of what the Bible *says*, but because of what it does *not* say. I know of no better example of it than this. What can we know? What can we believe? Well, let's see.

We can believe the Bible, my friend, and there are *two* things about Christ's return that are made unmistakably clear in the Scriptures:

(1) He is coming. You can be skeptical about these date-setters and their fantasies, but you must not be skeptical about this. He is coming and

(2) no man knows the day or the hour when the Lord will return.

Jesus himself said, "Of that day and hour knoweth no man, no, not the angels of heaven, but my Father only" (Matthew 24:36). And in Mark's account, it is recorded that Jesus said even He, the Son of God Himself, did not know (Luke 13:32). Now you can know that. And the next time some fellow comes across the stage saying he has it all figured out, or he has the latest word from heaven on the subject and sets a date, you will know not to be taken in. The Bible also says:

> When a prophet speaketh in the name of the Lord, if the thing follow not, nor come to pass, that is the thing which the Lord hath not spoken, but the prophet hath spoken it presumptuously: thou shalt not be afraid of him (Deuteronomy 18:22).

Our text says that "the day of the Lord will come as a thief in the night." There are other Scriptures that say the same thing—meaning, of course, that He will come at the least expected time, without warning. Jesus said:

> Watch therefore: for ye know not what hour your Lord doth come. But know this, that if the goodman of the house had known in what watch the thief would come, he would have watched, and would not have suffered his house to be broken up. Therefore be ye also ready: for in such an hour as ye think not the Son of man cometh (Matthew 24:42-44).

A thief never gives you a clue that he is coming over to burglarize your house. The message is "readiness," my friend. Get ready; stay ready; be ready when He comes!

We can know from the Bible that the glorious return of Christ will not be a quiet occasion witnessed only by a few, but that it will be heralded by the shout of angels and the sound of trumpets and every eye shall see Him! First Thessalonians 4:16 says, "For the Lord himself shall descend from heaven with a shout, with the voice of the archangel, and with the trump of God." And Revelation 1:7 tells us, "Behold, he cometh with clouds; and every eye shall see him, and they also which pierced him: and all kindreds of the earth shall wail because of him. Even so, Amen."

We can know from the Scriptures that when our Lord returns, that will be the end and God will be "all in all." First Corinthians 15:22-28 says:

> As in Adam all die, even so in Christ shall all be made alive. But every man in his own order: Christ the firstfruits; afterward they that are Christ's at his coming. Then cometh the end, when he shall have delivered up the kingdom to God, even the Father; when he shall have put down all rule and all authority and power.... And when all things shall be subdued unto him, then shall the Son also himself be subject unto him that put all things under him, that God may be all in all.

We can know, because the Bible says so, that at the coming of Christ, the dead will be raised, both the righteous and the wicked will be raised—at the same time. Jesus promised it in John 5:26-28. He said:

> For as the Father hath life in himself; so hath he given to the Son to have life in himself; and hath given him authority to execute judgment also, because he is the Son of man. Marvel not at this, [He said] for the hour is coming, in the which all that are in the graves shall hear his voice, and shall come forth; they that have done good, unto the resurrection of life; and they that have done evil, unto the resurrection of damnation.

We can know because the Bible declares it, that when Christ comes, the living saints will be changed "in a moment in the twinkling of an eye" and taken in their new bodies to live in glory with the Lord—forever (I Corinthians 15:51, 52; I Thessalonians 4:13-18).

We can know from II Peter 3:10, when the Lord comes, the earth and everything in it will be destroyed. The verse simply says:

> The day of the Lord will come as a thief in the night; in the which the heavens shall pass away with a great noise, and the elements shall melt with fervent heat, the earth also and the works that are therein shall be burned up.

Finally, we can know that on that day all men will appear before the great Judge of the universe and will give account for their lives. Jesus himself said in Matthew 25:31-33:

> When the Son of man shall come in his glory, and all the holy angels with him, then shall he sit upon the throne of his glory: and before him shall be gathered all nations: and he shall separate them one from another, as a shepherd divideth his sheep from the goats: and he shall set the sheep on his right hand, but the goats on the left.

He has not told us when that will be or given us any signs, so we must get ready, stay ready, and be ready. Are you, my friend? I would hope you would confess Him today and put Him on in baptism without delay.

No, my friend, you did not miss the rapture or the return of Christ on September thirteenth. It did not happen. But the second coming of Christ is going to be a great day! It is going to be a glorious day for the Christian. Some of the New Testament disciples did not want to die before the Lord returned because they wanted to be living at that moment. They were afraid that the dead saints would be at a disadvantage. But the apostle Paul wrote them two letters (the letters to the Thessalonians) to dispel that notion. Of course, it will be a dreadful and fearful day for the unbeliever and the scoffer.

It is this hope of His coming to receive His own to glory that inspires the Christian to live for Him every day. The things of this temporal world become less and less important in view of the great truth of the eternal nature of heaven. Such a hope takes away many of the tears on the death of a loved one who is a Christian too. When we stand beside the open grave of the deceased Christian, we have the hope that at our Lord's command, when He comes again, these remains will be changed into a glorious body and taken into the celestial city to live with God, Christ, and all the redeemed forever.

Well, I want that hope when it comes time to take that step out of this world into the next, don't you? It is in Christ, my friend. I hope you will get your life turned around in repentance and be baptized into Him at once. God bless and keep you. I love you.

QUESTIONS FOR CLASS DISCUSSION

1. Discuss the general dispensational-premillennialist doctrine of "the rapture."
2. Where is it found in the Scripture? What passage is *usually* used as a proof-text for the rapture doctrine?
3. Do Christians believe in the return of Christ?
4. What of those who say they know when Christ will come? Name some of those who have set dates for it. Shall we believe them? Why?
5. List all the things you can that a Christian can know about the second coming of Christ.
6. In I Thessalonians 4:16, what will happen *first*? Then what?
7. What is the important and relevant question for us concerning the second coming of Jesus?

4

Armageddon, the End of Time?

Revelation 3:10

Because thou hast kept the word of my patience, I also will keep thee from the hour of temptation, which shall come upon all the world, to try them that dwell upon the earth.

Wouldn't you know it? With all the military build up and activity in the Middle East, every self-styled prophet in America has boarded his soap box to predict "the battle of Armageddon" and the "end of the world." For almost a century now, every such political crisis has unleashed a flood of "prophecy" which is alleged to be direct communication from God, yet all the prophets have a different story. There is hardly to be found any two of them who are saying the same thing.

It seems to me, if God prophesied these events in Ezekiel, Daniel, or Revelation, *and that is what those prophecies are about*, they have been there all this time and it is as they claim—to be speaking by the Holy Ghost—they would all be speaking the same thing and they would have been saying it before now. Wouldn't you think so? And why is it that none of them saw Saddam Hussein as the principal figure in the prophecies of the "end of time" until his sudden invasion of Kuwait and the military response of other nations? Before that they said those same prophesies referred to Nassar Arafat or Mr.

Kadafee of Libya or President Hussein of Jordan or even Henry Kissinger.

Well, it might have been expected. Political developments in recent weeks resulting in the military activity in Saudi Arabia have triggered the wildest imagination of some of the sensationalist prophets with all kinds of fantasies concerning the rapture, the battle of Armageddon, the time of great tribulation, and the end of time. It is amazing though that the Bible says so little about some of those things. This leads us to the conclusion that they are but mere fantasies.

Some people wonder how modern prophets can preach so much about things of which the Bible says so little. For example, Revelation 16:16 is the only verse in all the Bible in which the word *Armageddon* appears. Beginning with verse 12, the passage says:

> And the sixth angel poured out his vial upon the great river Euphrates; and the water thereof was dried up, that the way of the kings of the east might be prepared. And I saw three unclean spirits like frogs come out of the mouth of the dragon, and out of the mouth of the beast, and out of the mouth of the false prophet. For they are the spirits of devils, working miracles, which go forth unto the kings of the earth and of the whole world, to gather them to the battle of that great day of God Almighty. Behold, I come as a thief. Blessed is he that watcheth, and keepeth his garments, lest he walk naked, and they see his shame. And he gathered them together into a place called in the Hebrew tongue Armageddon.

Only once does *Armageddon* appear in the Bible—just once and no more. It may be you are thinking, "Oh, it couldn't be; there just has to be more in the Scriptures about it than this one verse, or well, there is an awful lot of fabrication going on in some preaching."

Well, let's look into it. The word *Armageddon* in this verse (King James Version) is actually *Harmageddon* and it literally means "mountain or hill of Megiddo." In the days when John wrote the book of Revelation, that little mountain or hill or knoll was only about seventy feet high. Located in the central section of the land of Palestine, looking down over the rich, fertile Valley of Jezreel, which took its name, and being the crossroads of the trade routes from Egypt and Babylon and Syria, it was of strategic importance. Whoever controlled Megiddo would control the trade routes and all the area around about.

It goes without saying, then, that Megiddo played an important role in history and witnessed a succession of conquerors: Egyptians, Canaanites, Philistines, Israelites, Assyrians, Persians, Greeks, and Romans. Many, many great battles were fought there. In modern times, 1918, the Allied Forces under General Allenby entered Northern Palestine through the Megiddo Pass to wrest it from the Turkish forces, after which the British commander was named Viscount Allenby of Megiddo.

Megiddo is first mentioned in the Bible in Joshua 12:21. It was during the conquest of Canaan, under the leadership of Joshua, that the Israelites won a temporary victory over the king of Megiddo. When Joshua divided the land among the tribes, Megiddo was assigned to the tribe of Manasseh (Joshua 17:11). However, because Joshua did not completely drive the Canaanites out of the city, the victory was only temporary and the Canaanites actually controlled it during the period of conquest.

During the reign of the judges, there were some interesting battles that were fought there. In the days of Deborah, for example, the northern tribes of Israel, under Barak, fought the Canaanites under Sisera by the waters of Megiddo and defeated them (Judges 5:19). In the seventh chapter of Judges there is the story of Gideon and his select army of only three hundred men whom God had chosen who defeated the hosts of Midianites here at Megiddo. You see, so far as Israel is concerned, they won some of their great victories on this now famous battlefield.

Chapter 4

They also suffered some great defeats at Megiddo. It was there that Saul and Jonathan were killed in battle (I Samuel 31). King Ahaziah of Judah died there after he was struck by an arrow from the bow of Jehu, king of Israel (II Kings 9). Good King Josiah was sorely wounded in a battle with Necho, king of Egypt at Megiddo, and died before he arrived in Jerusalem.

I have said all that about Megiddo so that you can see it was a historical battlefield, the scene of some great victories, but also some disastrous defeats. It came to be a symbol of bloody conflict and devastating loss. It is one of the great battlefields of the world, like Waterloo, Dunkirk, Normandy, or the Texas Alamo. Great kings and mighty armies were vanquished at Megiddo.

Now when John came to write in this book of Revelation about a great conflict of some kind, he employed this symbolic language. He is not talking about a particular war, physical combat involving hundreds of millions of people in any period of history, not in the first century, not in the twentieth century or the twenty-first century, not when Christ came the first time, not when He comes again. He is using it in a symbolic way.

Remember that as we look at Revelation 16:13. John said, "I saw three unclean spirits *like* frogs come out of the mouth of the dragon, and out of the mouth of the beast, and out of the mouth of the false prophet." Did you notice the symbolism? These were not real frogs; they were like frogs. Neither was the dragon real nor the beast nor the false prophet.

Now right here in all of this symbolism are we going to force a literal interpretation on Armageddon? Of course not! If all of that context is symbolism, then Armageddon in the context is also going to be symbolic. John is not predicting a real war in the Middle East that will mark the end of the age, the return of Christ, and finally the end of the world.

We have an expression "he met his waterloo" meaning someone suffered defeat. Or we may speak prophetically: "If

John does as he is planning, it will be his waterloo," meaning the results will be catastrophic. In a similar way, to the people of John's day the expression, "gathering at Armageddon," signified making a final stand. A person would no more have to literally go to the hill of Megiddo to make his final stand than he would have to go literally to Waterloo to suffer total defeat. The gathering of the kings together at Armageddon in Revelation 16:15 is figurative and does not predict a literal battle that will bring an end of the age and usher in the millennial reign of Jesus in Jerusalem, but a final stand.

For an understanding of any passage of Scripture, we must interpret it within its context. No book, or any part of a book of the Bible, should ever be interpreted to mean something which it was not intended to mean when (and to whom) it was originally written. Revelation was written along toward the end of the first century. It was of current interest and relevance at that time. It was appropriate, was applicable, and had meaning for the people of that time. Surely no one would take the position that the book of Revelation was meaningless to the people to whom it was written in the first century.

Well, the very first sentence of the book says, "The Revelation of Jesus Christ, which God gave unto him, to shew unto his servants things which *must shortly come to pass.*" And verse 3 says, "*The time is at hand.*" So the message of the book of Revelation concerns something that was about to happen *then*—in the lifetime of the people living—and it was of critical interest and concern to servants of the Lord at that time.

To force an interpretation on the book of Revelation or any part of it which would make it refer to Saddam Hussein, Iraq, Russia, the United States, or any person or event of the twentieth century would render it meaningless to the people to whom it was written and completely miss the message of the entire book. Revelation is a prophecy of something that was to "shortly come to pass." The time was at hand.

John was exiled on the island of Patmos for preaching Christ. Other Christians scattered throughout the world were likewise suffering cruel persecution at the hands of Rome. And our Lord used John in exile to write the message of Revelation to comfort and encourage those fellow-Christians in the face of greater oppression and greater trials which were soon to come upon them. That would be their "gathering at Armageddon." The message of Revelation, therefore, is one of comfort and encouragement for those disciples suffering under those conditions. And its real meaning for us is the same. It is a message of encouragement to live and to die for Christ. It is a message of hope and victory over the forces who oppose us.

The next verse says:

> For they are the spirits of devils, working miracles, which go forth unto the kings of the earth and of the whole world, to gather them to the battle of that great day of God Almighty.

In Old Testament prophecy, "the great day of God Almighty" always meant the time of the destruction of some political entity or empire. And that is what it means here. Now any passage must also be interpreted in the light of, in the time frame, and in keeping with the purpose of the book in which it is written. It was an event of immediate concern at that time. Rome was to come to its "gathering at Armageddon."

The false prophet in the passage symbolizes the false religion of Roman emperor worship. History records the severity of the persecution inflicted by Rome upon the Christians who refused to bow down to the emperor or to worship him. They worshiped God only. Under the heel of the oppressor, they cried. "Oh Lord, how long, how long must we suffer so?" And the Lord says that it will not be long. In chapter 16, He says there is coming a great "showdown," a "gathering at Armageddon," as it were, and Rome will fall. Rome did fall and the prophecy was fulfilled.

Perhaps you noticed a moment ago that I passed over verse 15. That was not a mistake; it was intentional. In the American Standard Version, that verse is in parenthesis so we did it no injustice to hold it until now. It says, "Behold, I come as a thief, blessed is he that watcheth, and keepeth his garments, lest he walk naked, and they see his shame." Christ is coming for His own. And the idea is that we be prepared. He did not say He was giving us a lot of signs, a countdown to His coming. He said He would come as a thief. A thief does not give you a call to say I will be over at three o'clock in the morning to rob and destroy. As a matter of fact, every time Jesus mentioned His coming, He said it would be at an unexpected time. Since no one knows the day or the hour of His coming, each of us should live every day as though *it* is the day of Christ and keep our garments, lest He find us unprepared and in shame.

Such preparation is in being a Christian, having been saved by the blood of Jesus and being faithful to the very end. In the first chapter of Revelation (verse 5) John says, Christ "loved us and washed us from our sins in His own blood." To the Christians in Ephesus (Revelation 2:7), Christ said:

> He that hath an ear, let him hear what the Spirit saith unto the churches: to him that overcometh will I give to eat of the tree of life, which is in the midst of the paradise of God.

And to His disciples in Smyrna, He said:

> Be thou faithful unto death, and I will give thee a crown of life. He that hath an ear, let him hear what the Spirit saith unto the churches; he that overcometh shall not be hurt of the second death" (Revelation 2:10, 11).

My friend, are you washed in the blood of the lamb of God? Are you faithful? Those are the critical thoughts of this passage. If you must answer in the negative, I pray you will do as Saul of Tarsus was told: "Arise and be baptized and wash away thy sins, calling on the name of the Lord" (Acts 22:16) and that, as he was, you will remain faithful to your commitment until death. If we may assist you in rendering such obedience to Christ, we would love to hear from you at once.

Chapter 4

Please remember when you study any passage of Scripture that it must not be forced to mean something it did not mean to the people to whom it was addressed. If Revelation 16 refers to current events in the Middle East, it would have been absolutely meaningless to the people of the first century and all subsequent generations until now. It referred to a "showdown" with the persecuting power of Rome and the Christians would win—so be faithful! Rome fell. The Christians won. The message is one of encouragement, hope, and victory to Christians of any generation under severe trial and suffering. God bless you. I love you.

QUESTIONS FOR CLASS DISCUSSION

1. How many times does the word *Armageddon* appear in our English versions of the Bible? Where?
2. What is the significance of "the battle of Armageddon" in the dispensational-premillennial theory?
3. To what does "Armageddon" (Harmageddon) refer?
4. Locate Megiddo on the map. Why was it such a strategic place?
5. Name some historic battles fought there.
6. What did "gathering at Armageddon" mean?
7. Is the battle of Armageddon to be taken literally now? Why? What does it mean?

5

Daniel 2 and the Kingdom of Christ

Daniel 2:44

And in the days of these kings shall the God of heaven set up a kingdom, which shall never be destroyed: and the kingdom shall not be left to other people, but it shall break in pieces and consume all these kingdoms, and it shall stand for ever.

Prophecy is one of the strongest proofs we have of the authenticity of the Bible as the inspired word of God. If just one of the Bible prophecies can be proven inaccurate, or if it can be proven not to have come to pass just as the prophet said it would, there is absolutely no reason to take the Bible seriously or to accept it as an inspired guide. But if those prophecies of the Old Testament were fulfilled as the prophets spoke them, the Bible is confirmed by them as divine revelation and must be taken seriously as our rule of faith and practice.

It has been said, "Daniel is the most important witness among all the prophets to the credibility of the prophets in general and of divine revelation and the Christian religion in particular." The prophecies of Daniel are some of the most misunderstood and misapplied Scriptures used by modern prophets who use them to try to establish a millennial reign of Christ in Jerusalem when He comes. In this message, we are going to examine Daniel's prophecy of the establishment of the kingdom of Christ in Daniel 2.

In 607 B.C., Nebuchadnezzar, king of Babylon, having besieged Jerusalem and made its king tributary, carried away a number of captives. Among them was the prophet Daniel. By the providence of God, Daniel gained a place of respect and eminence in Babylon. It was in the second year of King Nebuchadnezzar's reign that the king had a dream that really troubled him, but he could not remember it and he did not know what it meant. He called all his magicians, astrologers, sorcerers, and the Chaldeans and demanded of them that they tell him the dream and the interpretation or be cut in pieces. But, they said:

> There is not a man upon the earth that can shew the king's matter: therefore there is no king, lord, nor ruler, that asked such things at any magician, or astrologer, or Chaldean. . . . [So] the decree went forth that the wise men should be slain; and they sought Daniel and his fellows to be slain (Daniel 2:10-13).

Daniel asked for some time. He and his friends prayed about it; God answered their prayers; they thanked God and praised Him. Then Daniel told the king the dream and the interpretation.

In his dream the king saw a great image, exceedingly luminous and terrible in appearance with a head of fine gold, breast and arms of silver, belly and thighs of brass, legs of iron, and its feet and toes of iron and clay. While he gazed on this image, he saw a stone cut out without hands which smote the image on his feet of iron and clay and broke them in pieces. And the stone became a great mountain and filled the whole earth. Can you imagine the astonishment of old King Nebuchadnezzar when Daniel had detailed his dream as he did? And he must have been as confident and eager as he was surprised to hear the interpretation, knowing that any man who could so exactly reveal the dream could just as accurately give the interpretation. He must have been thinking, if he was not saying,

Daniel 2 and the Kingdom of Christ

"Hurry on young man with the interpretation."
In verse 36, Daniel says:

> This is the dream, and we will tell the interpretation thereof before the king. Thou, O king, art a king of kings: for the God of heaven hath given thee a kingdom, power, and strength, and glory. And wheresoever the children of men dwell, the beasts of the field and the fowls of the heaven hath he given into thine hand, and hath made thee ruler over them all. Thou art this head of gold. And after thee shall arise another kingdom inferior to thee, and another third kingdom of brass, which shall bear rule over all the earth. And the fourth kingdom shall be strong as iron: forasmuch as iron breaketh in pieces and subdueth all things: and as iron that breaketh all these, shall it break in pieces and bruise. And whereas thou sawest the feet and toes, part of potters' clay and part of iron, the kingdom shall be divided; but there shall be in it of the strength of the iron, forasmuch as thou sawest the iron mixed with miry clay. And as the toes of the feet were part of iron and part of clay, so the kingdom shall be partly strong, and partly broken. And whereas thou sawest iron mixed with miry clay, they shall mingle themselves with the seed of men: but they shall not cleave one to another, even as iron is not mixed with clay.
>
> And in the days of these kings shall the God of heaven set up a kingdom, which shall never be destroyed: and the kingdom shall not be left to other people, but it shall break in pieces and consume all these kingdoms, and it shall stand for ever. Forasmuch as thou sawest that the stone was cut out of the mountain without hands, and that it brake in pieces the iron, the brass, the clay, the silver, and the gold; the great God hath made known to the king what shall come to pass hereafter: and the dream is certain, and the interpretation thereof sure (Daniel 2:36-45).

Indeed, Nebuchadnezzar was blessed, being privileged to know of God's plan for the affairs of men for centuries to come.

And the Scripture says that he answered Daniel, "Of a truth it is, that your God is a God of gods" (Daniel 2:47).

The mighty empire of Babylon over which Nebuchadnezzar then reigned was represented by the head of fine gold. While this was good news to him, it was also bad news. Because, despite the glory and power of the great empire over which he ruled, the message was clear: it would one day fall to a power that was inferior—to that one represented by the breast and arms of silver.

Cyrus the Mede and Darius the Persian combined their forces against Babylon and conquered it and in 536 B.C. formed the empire of the Medes and Persians, the second world power represented in the image of Nebuchadnezzar's dream by the breast and arms of silver.

But the image projected the rise of another monarchy to succeed that of the Medes and Persians. It was represented by the belly and thighs of brass. Students of both secular and inspired history know it to be the Macedonian rule under the brief reign of Alexander the Great. Alexander defeated Darius III at Arbela in October 331 B.C. and thus terminated the Persian Monarchy. Because of Alexander's continued military conquests, he did fulfill the prophecy to "rule over all the earth" (Daniel 2:39), and he sat down and wept because there were no more worlds to conquer. Following a prolonged drinking spree, Alexander came down with a fever and died. He was 33. The Macedonian Empire was unable to survive his death.

In 34 B.C., there arose out of the ruins of these three world empires, the fourth represented in the image of Nebuchadnezzar's dream by the legs of iron and the feet of iron and clay (Daniel 2:40-43). Adam Clark says:

> These two legs of iron became absorbed in the Roman government, which also partook of the iron nature: strong, military, and extensive in its victories; and by its various conquests united to and amalgamated with itself various nations, some strong, and some weak, so as to be fitly represented in the symbolical image by feet and toes, partly of iron and partly of clay.

Daniel 2 and the Kingdom of Christ

These were the four world powers in Daniel's prophecy.

Now, the critical point is in verse 44:

> In the days of these kings shall the God of heaven set up a kingdom, which shall never be destroyed: and the kingdom shall not be left to other people, but it shall break in pieces and consume all these kingdoms, and it shall stand forever.

This a direct reference to the establishment of the kingdom of the Messiah. It was to be established in the days of the Roman kings, somewhere between 34 B.C. and A.D. 476.

One of America's foremost premillennial dispensationalists says of that verse:

> The last part of Nebuchadnezzer's dream foretold the dramatic establishment of the kingdom of God after the last of the four empires and their successors have been destroyed.

But that is not what Daniel said, is it? He said, "*In the days* of these kings," not after. You see, in order to apply Old Testament prophecy to current world events, there must be a perversion of the Scripture. That perversion must be subtle, and it is. So much so that if we are not very careful, such perversion will go unnoticed.

Another who has made millions with his books and broadcasts on supposed prophecies on the state of the world today, avoids the force of Daniel's statement, "In the days of these kings," by saying that the Roman Empire became a world power (34 B.C. - A.D. 476), then disappeared, but that it will be revived just before the return of Christ at which time the kingdom of God will be established and Daniel's prophecy will be fulfilled.

There is even suggestion that the work and rule of such men as Justinian in A.D. 554, Charlemagne in A.D. 800, Napoleon in the late eighteenth century, even Hitler's Third Reich, the formation of the European Common Market, and more recently the new United States of Europe as attempts at revival of

Rome, or Rome Phase II. It is interesting to note that when the European Common Market did not materialize as they prophesied it would do in the 1980s, they reset the date for 1992 for the establishment of a "United States of Europe" to fulfill Daniel's prophecies. We shall see.

It is impossible to examine every theory individually, but the more traditional view among premillennialists is that Christ did come to establish His reign or kingdom, but He was rejected and crucified, His plans were thwarted, so He revised the plan and will do so at His second coming.

Well, was the prophecy of Daniel 2:44, "In the days of these kings, shall the God of heaven set up a kingdom which shall never be destroyed," fulfilled in the days of the Roman kings? "No," they tell us, "it was not." Then the Bible is not true, my friend. It is just that plain and simple.

Now let us take a quick look at the New Testament. And do not be surprised if we come upon some passages that have to do with the kingdom of Daniel's prophecies. The first chapter of the New Testament records the birth of Jesus. The Stone which was hewn out of the mountain without hands, which smote the image in the feet and destroyed it and filled all the earth, is Christ. I know of no one who denies that the Stone was Christ. The second chapter of Matthew tells of the decree of Herod that all children two years old and under be put to death. The third chapter opens saying, "In those days came John the Baptist, preaching in the wilderness of Judea, and saying, Repent ye: for the kingdom of heaven is at hand." Judea, where our Savior was born, was a province of the Roman Empire. Herod, who received his appointment and power from Rome, had reigned at the time of the birth of Jesus thirty-four years. And the Scripture says, "In those days came John the Baptist, preaching in the wilderness of Judea, and saying, Repent ye: for the kingdom of heaven is at hand."

The next chapter says, "From that time Jesus began to preach, and to say, Repent: for the kingdom of heaven is at hand" (Matthew 4:17). He even went so far as to say, "I tell

Daniel 2 and the Kingdom of Christ

you of a truth, there be some standing here, which shall not taste of death, till they see the kingdom of God" (Luke 9:27). Jesus commissioned His apostles to preach "the kingdom of heaven is at hand" (Matthew 10:7). He sent the seventy out to say, "The kingdom of God is come nigh unto you" (Luke 10:9). Did it ever happen? Is it yet to be? If the kingdom of Christ does not exist now, all of those teachings were false.

But they are not false because Paul wrote the Christians at Colossae that God "hath translated us into the kingdom of his dear Son" (Colossians 1:13). Are we translated into a nonentity when we are saved? Hebrews 12:28 says, "Wherefore we receiving a kingdom which cannot be moved, let us have grace, whereby we may serve God acceptably with reverence and godly fear." Have we received a non-existent? John, exiled on Patmos, was in the kingdom (Revelation 1:9). Was he in non-reality?

No, Christ the Messiah did fulfill Daniel 2:44 on the first Jewish Pentecost following His resurrection. And today He reigns over all the kingdoms of the world as "Lord of lords and King of kings" (Revelation 17:14). "And he hath on his vesture and on his thigh a name written, KING OF KINGS, AND LORD OF LORDS" (Revelation 19:16).

Premillennialists have failed to recognize His kingdom because of their materialistic theology and because the kingdom of Christ is not a political force with conquering armies. It is a spiritual reign of love, joy, peace, longsuffering, gentleness, goodness, faith, meekness, and self-control (Galatians 5:22, 23).

The Bible says in Romans 14:17: "The kingdom of God is ... righteousness, and peace, and joy in the Holy Ghost." And you, my friend, should be a citizen of it. You can be simply by putting yourself under the command of King Jesus in loving, trusting obedience, in repentance and baptism in His name, to follow him and live for him all the days of your life. Why not do it now? God bless you. I love you.

QUESTIONS FOR CLASS DISCUSSION

1. Why is the fulfillment of Old Testament prophecy so important to the reliability of the entire Bible?
2. Relate Nebuchadnezzar's dream.
3. Tell the interpretation of the dream.
4. What was to happen during the fourth kingdom?
5. Did it happen? How do you know?
6. How do some people subtly evade the force of "In the days of those kings"?
7. What New Testament proof do we have that the prophecy was fulfilled as spoken?
8. Why do dispensational premillennialists not recognize the present existence of the kingdom (reign) of Christ?

6

Israel and the Land Promise

> *Genesis 12:1-3*
>
> *Now the Lord had said unto Abram, Get thee out of thy country, and from thy kindred, and from thy father's house, unto a land that I will shew thee: and I will make of thee a great nation, and I will bless thee, and make thy name great; and thou shalt be a blessing: and I will bless them that bless thee, and curse him that curseth thee: and in thee shall all families of the earth be blessed.*

For more than a century there has been widespread interest in the return of the Jews to the land of Palestine. Since the formation of the State of Israel in 1948, speculation has been especially great and has intensified again by Operation Desert Storm. Self-styled "prophets" see these things as fulfillment of the promise made to Abraham which must come to pass before "the rapture," Armageddon, the end of the world, and the return of Christ to establish His millennial reign in Jerusalem.

These things are so widely taught in American religion that they are just assumed by most folks to be true without examination. For example, I am holding a copy of the Saturday church page in our newspaper a few weeks ago. The "Bible Lesson" of the week is headlined, "God Is Keeping His Promise in Israel," in which the author affirms (without proof) that the current migration of Jews to the land of Palestine is God's preparatory work to send the Messiah to establish His utopian reign of peace on earth. What he fails to observe is that God fulfilled those prophecies when He sent the Messiah, whom the Jews rejected—and crucified.

The idea is strong, even among some leaders of world governments, that the land of Palestine belongs to the Jews by right of the promise made to Abraham and that nations who oppose Israel's occupation of those lands are actually opposing God and will be brought to naught. Some of the "peace accords" and international treaties in recent years have been influenced by these assumptions.

Well, what about all of this? What does the Bible actually say? Whether you are aware of it or not, it is having a direct bearing on much of your life. We hope not to add to the confusion of speculation that abounds, but to search the Scriptures to learn what God actually says about it all. The Bible and only the Bible speaks the will of God. Anyone who says he has another message from God comes under the anathema of God and we should beware of him (Galatians 1:8, 9).

The promise made to Abraham was basically threefold:

(1) God would make his descendants into a great nation.

(2) He would give them the land of Canaan in which to dwell. And

(3) He would bless *all* nations with the birth of the Savior through Abraham's seed.

The promise is first found in Genesis 12:2-4 on the occasion of the call of Abraham:

> Now the Lord had said unto Abram, Get thee out of thy country, and from thy kindred, and from thy father's house, unto a land that I will shew thee: and I will make of thee a great nation, and I will bless thee, and make thy name great; and thou shalt be a blessing: and I will bless them that bless thee, and curse him that curseth thee: and in thee shall all families of the earth be blessed.

It is found again in chapter 17 where there is more said about the land part of the covenant, and since that is the focus of our study today, let us take a look at verses 7 and 8. God said to Abraham:

> I will establish my covenant between me and thee and thy seed after thee in their generations for an everlasting covenant, to be a God unto thee, and to thy seed after thee. And I will give unto thee, and to thy seed after thee, the land wherein thou art a stranger, all the land of Canaan, for an everlasting possession: and I will be their God.

However, in the fifteenth chapter God told Abraham that they would not occupy the land until after a period of four hundred years of servitude in a strange land, because the iniquity of the Amorites who lived in Canaan was not yet full. But in the fourth generation, they would be brought into Canaan, and even the limits or boundaries of the inheritance are set forth.

Abraham was the father of Ishmael by Hagar and the father of Isaac by Sarah. Ishmael became the father of the Arab peoples. Isaac had twin sons, Jacob and Esau. Esau is the father of the Edomite nation. Jacob's name was changed to Israel from whom the Israelites receive their name. He had twelve sons and these were the heads of the twelve tribes of Israel. One of the sons of Jacob, Joseph, was sold by his brothers to the Ishmaelites and Midianites in Dothan, who took him to Egypt where he was sold into slavery. Later he was made next to the king in power and ruled as governor, "Prime Minister" in modern terminology. After some time, Joseph sent for Israel and all his family and they came into Egypt to live.

They were in bondage in Egypt for 430 years (Exodus 12:40) and, under the leadership of Moses, they were delivered out of slavery just as God promised, and set out for the promised land. Moses died and, under the leadership of Joshua, they crossed over Jordan and possessed the land. When Joshua was about to go the way of all the earth, in his farewell speech to Israel in Joshua 21:43, he declared his mission accomplished. He said, "And the Lord gave unto Israel all the land which he sware unto their fathers; and they possessed it, and dwelt in it." God had fulfilled His land promise to Abraham.

Israel was ruled by judges for a period of about 450 years until they demanded a king like the nations about them and God gave them Saul. His reign of forty years was followed by the forty-year reign of David. The kingdom then came to the zenith of its power and glory under the reign of King Solomon, whose death terminated that grand period of the United Kingdom and ushered in a time of trouble. Division immediately developed between Judah and Israel and the ten northern tribes seceded, establishing their capital in Shechem under Jeroboam. Rehoboam, Solomon's son, ruled the two tribes of the Southern Kingdom (I Kings 12 and 13). The kingdom of Israel went into captivity to Assyria about 721 B.C. The kingdom of Judah existed from 930 B.C. to 587 B.C. and went into captivity to Babylon—*because* they forsook God and worshiped idols.

Jeremiah prophesied during the last days of the kingdom of Judah in 587 B.C. He told the people God had sent His servants, the prophets, to them to turn them from their evil and idolatrous ways, but they would not hearken or incline their ears. For that reason Jeremiah said God would send Nebuchadnezzar, king of Babylon against them and utterly destroy them and the whole land would be a desolation for seventy years. *Then*, God would return them to the land (Jeremiah 25:4-14). So the prophets told of a return to the land, often called "the restoration prophecies."

In II Chronicles 36:22, 23 the Scripture says:

> Now in the first year of Cyrus king of Persia, *that the word of the Lord spoken by the mouth of Jeremiah might be accomplished*, the Lord stirred up the spirit of Cyrus king of Persia, that he made a proclamation throughout all his kingdom, and put it also in writing, saying, Thus saith Cyrus king of Persia, All the kingdoms of the earth hath the Lord God of heaven given me; and he hath charged me to build him an house in Jerusalem, which is in Judah, who is there among you of all his people? The Lord his God be with him, and let him go up.

So Israel was returned to the land. The city and temple were rebuilt. God's promises and prophecies had been fulfilled.

Now we have traced the history of Israel and her relationship to the land of Palestine as it is in the Bible. God promised it to Abraham and his seed for an inheritance. Israel entered the land, possessed the land—all of it—and dwelt in it. Because they forgot God and served idols, God removed them from the land, but He promised to return them to it after seventy years, which He did, and fulfilled every Old Testament promise and prophecy regarding their possession of the land.

My friend, there is not one single Old Testament prophecy concerning Israel's possession of Canaan that is applicable to current events. The prophecies had to mean what was intended when the prophets spoke them. If they referred to those historical events, they cannot be made to mean the present status of Israel. They were promised the land. They occupied it. They were driven from it. They were returned to it. And they were living there at the time of the birth of Jesus, but they were not self-governing.

When Herod the Great died in 4 B.C., his kingdom was divided among his three sons: Archelaus received Judea; Philip, Thraconitis; and Antipas, Galilee. In A.D. 25 Pontius Pilate was appointed procurator of Judea by emperor Tiberius and it was during this time that Jesus was crucified. In A.D. 41, Agrippa I, a grandson of Herod the Great, was elevated to the throne of Judea. After his death in A.D. 44, Judea had a series of procurators whose bad government eventually led to an outburst of popular feelings and hostilities. Jerusalem was in turmoil and the country prepared for the coming struggle; a war that was to end in the most devastating and complete destruction Jerusalem had ever suffered. In A.D. 67, Cestius Gallus, the governor of Syria, tried to intervene but was defeated. The illustrious General Vespasian was dispatched to crush the Jewish revolt. After two years of preparation, all was ready to undertake the siege of Jerusalem. Nero died and Vespasian was declared his successor, and his son Titus assumed command of the campaign against the Jews. The siege of Jerusalem lasted five months and the story of its horrors furnished one of the darkest pages in history. One part of the city after another was stormed, the temple was burned, and those inhabitants who survived the massacre were enslaved and carried away captive.

Since A.D. 70 there has been no national Israel and no national occupation of the land until the order of the United Nations in 1948. While that order is supposed by some to fulfill God's promise to Abraham, it does not. That promise was completely fulfilled in the Old Testament history we have cited.

However, you may be wondering about that word *everlasting*, in the land promise. What of the "everlasting" nature of the covenant with Abraham? The *Theological Wordbook of the Old Testament*, (Volume II, pages 672, 673) says of the word *everlasting*:

> That neither the Hebrew nor the Greek word in its self contains the idea of endlessness is shown both by the fact that they *sometimes* refer to events or conditions that occurred at a definite point in the past, and also by the fact that sometimes it is thought desirable to repeat the word, not merely saying "forever," but "forever and ever." Both words (everlasting and forever) came to be used to refer to a long age or period. . . . Meaning then, that the covenant was not to be understood as an "endless" one because of the word "everlasting," but one of a long age or period of time.

The New Testament says that Christ "came to his own [the Jews] and his own received him not" (John 1:11). When the Jews rejected Jesus as the Messiah and crucified Him, they committed the national crime for which they paid with national death. The Lord Himself taught in the parable of the wicked husbandmen in Matthew 21:33-46 that the kingdom was taken from the Jews and given to others. The Holy Spirit says to Christians:

> Unto you therefore which believe, he [Christ] is precious; but unto them which be disobedient, the stone which the builders disallowed, the same is made the

head of the corner, and a stone of stumbling, and a rock of offense, even to them which stumble at the word, being disobedient: whereunto also they were appointed. But ye are a chosen generation, a royal priesthood, an holy nation, a peculiar people; that ye should shew forth the praises of him who hath called you out of darkness into his marvelous light: which in time past were not a people, but are now the people of God (I Peter 2:7-9).

God's Israel is no longer a fleshly nation but a spiritual one. In the Old Testament, the Jews were His chosen people, but in the New Testament, the church is the chosen people of God. In the Old Testament, Israel was the holy nation, but in the New Testament, it is the church. In the Old Testament, Israel was the people of God's own possession, but in the New Testament, it is the church, purchased with the blood of Christ (Acts 20:28). Paul made it clear that:

Ye are all children of God by faith in Christ Jesus. For as many of you as have been baptized into Christ have put on Christ. There is neither Jew nor Greek, there is neither bond nor free, there is neither male nor female; for ye are all one in Christ. And if ye be Christ's, then are ye Abraham's seed, and heirs according to the promise (Galatians 3:26-29).

The Israel of today is not of Abraham's *seed*, but of Abraham's *faith.*

When Paul made his defense before Agrippa, he said:

And now I stand and am judged for the hope of the promise made of God unto our fathers: unto which promise our twelve tribes, instantly serving God day and night hope to come (Acts 26:6, 7).

Paul was *imprisoned* and *judged* for "the hope of Israel," which he said was based on the promise made to our fathers which the twelve tribes, he said, "hope to come." Obviously Paul's inspired understanding of that promise did not agree with the national hopes cherished by the Jews. It was for the hope of Israel that he was bound as a prisoner (Acts 28:20).

Do you think the Jews would have bound Paul and persecuted him as they did if he had preached that the hope of Israel was their *national restoration?* Of course not!

Those Old Testament prophecies of a national Israel were fulfilled in the Old Testament period, and the hope of Israel today lies in something else. What could it be? Well, the Scriptures tell us. It is the fulfillment of the promise made to Abraham that *"in thy seed shall all the nations of the earth be blessed,"* and the seed is Christ.

> For in Christ Jesus neither circumcision availeth anything, nor uncircumcision, but a new creature. And as many as walk according to this rule, peace be on them, and mercy, and upon the Israel of God (Galatians 6:15, 16).

Our concern for Israel is not a national restoration, but just as it is for all Gentile peoples too, their acceptance of Christ as Savior and Redeemer. God bless you. I love you.

QUESTIONS FOR CLASS DISCUSSION

1. Why has the land promise to Abraham become so interesting to preachers and politicians in the twentieth century?
2. Tell of God's promise to Abraham. Tell how all of it was fulfilled, even the land promise.
3. Who is the "father" of the Arab people?
4. Through whom do the Israelites trace their lineage to Abraham?
5. When were the Jews to return to Palestine?
6. What part of the land promise is applicable to world events of this century?
7. Who are God's "chosen people" today? How do you know?
8. What was the hope of Israel as preached by Paul?

7

Antichrist and the Mark of the Beast

I John 4:1-3

Beloved, believe not every spirit, but try the spirits whether they are of God: because many false prophets are gone out into the world. Hereby know ye the Spirit of God: Every spirit that confesseth that Jesus Christ is come in the flesh is of God: and every spirit that confesseth not that Jesus Christ is come in the flesh is not of God: and this is that spirit of antichrist, whereof ye have heard that it should come; and even now already is it in the world.

With world conditions as they are, we are hearing a lot of sensational speculation about "Antichrist and the Mark of the Beast." Some of it would be amusing if it were not so serious. The general idea is that Christ's return to the earth will be immediately preceded by the appearance of some powerful political personality, perhaps a dictator of world influence, who will make a dramatic appearance in history. One popular writer says:

> Overnight, he will become the by-word of the world. He is going to be distinguished as supernatural.... He will have a magnetic personality, be personally attractive, and a powerful speaker.

In the memory of many of us, popular prophets have pointed to Benito Mussolini, Adolf Hitler, Joseph Stalin, Nikita Kruschev, Fidel Castro, even former U. S. Secretary of State

Henry Kissinger, but most recently, as you would expect, to Saddam Hussein as the antichrist. Cox News Service reporter Hap Cawood says, "If you're buying any of these fantasies, you should get a money-back guarantee, because they don't last."

We have no private theory or interpretation to present or to defend, so we can approach the Scriptures objectively to see what they actually say (if anything) about these subjects.

I would like us to begin our study with reading every verse in the Bible that mentions *antichrist*. Fair enough? There are none in the Old Testament. And only in the epistles of John (I John and II John) are there any in the New Testament. What do they say:

> Little children, it is the last time: and as ye have heard that antichrist shall come, even now are there many antichrists; whereby we know that it is the last time (I John 2:18).

> Who is a liar but he that denieth that Jesus is the Christ? He is antichrist, that denieth the Father and the Son (I John 2:22).

> And every spirit that confesseth not that Jesus Christ is come in the flesh is not of God: and this is that spirit of antichrist, whereof ye have heard that it should come; and even now already is it in the world (I John 4:3).

> For many deceivers are entered into the world, who confess not that Jesus Christ is come in the flesh. This is a deceiver and an antichrist (II John 7).

Any passage of Scripture is more easily and accurately understood when it is studied within its context. To lift a verse out of its setting, to make it mean something it would not mean if considered in its setting, is to twist or pervert God's word. Those who practice that sort of thing are appropriately called "false teachers," and God Himself pronounces an anathema upon them (Galatians 1:7-9).

So what is the message of the only two epistles (letters) that mention an antichrist? Well, John, the last remaining apostle, was living in the Roman province of Ephesus and was much concerned about a disturbing problem that had arisen in the churches of that area; namely, some people (in the church) were teaching a new doctrine relative to the person of Jesus Christ. They denied that Jesus Christ was come in the flesh as was (is) generally taught. Such was factually a denial that Jesus Christ was the Messiah or Son of God. These people held that matter is something essentially lowly and impure, and refused to believe that Christ had taken human flesh.

They and the Gnostics, who were so called because of their claim to possess superior knowledge, taught that at Jesus' baptism, the divine Spirit (Christ) came upon Him but left Him before His crucifixion, so that while "Christ" was divine, "Jesus" was not. This heresy was disturbing the love and the fellowship of the churches. John, by the Holy Spirit, calls these people "liars" (I John 2:22), "false prophets" (I John 4:1), "deceivers" (II John 7) and "antichrists" (I John 4:3). And it does not sound anything remotely akin to what you are hearing today about the antichrist, does it?

In order to develop their theories, modern false prophets lift these verses about antichrist completely out of that setting and associate them with the "little horn" of Daniel 7, the "man of sin" of II Thessalonians 2, and the "beasts" of Revelation 13. It should be noticed, though, that neither the book of Revelation nor any other Bible book ever relates the antichrist with those passages. If we are to understand biblical teaching about antichrist, we must view it in John's setting and time.

From an examination of those four verses in which "antichrist" and "antichrists" are mentioned, we can learn:

(1) They existed in the past and present of John's day. First John 2:18 says, "Ye have heard that antichrist shall come, even now are there many antichrists." So John's readers must not look for a single mysterious figure in remote future years, but for many antichrists who "have come." In chapter 4 verse 3, he says this spirit of antichrist which you have heard must come, is now already in the world.

(2) There are "many antichrists," not one political ruler or dictator. Anyone who denies the deity and the incarnation of Jesus Christ is an antichrist.

(3) From the next verse (19), we learn that the antichrists "went out from us." They were former Christians who had left the faith, *not* some world political leader.

(4) The antichrists denied the deity of Jesus Christ (I John 2:22). *Anyone* who does so is an antichrist, whether in John's day or ours, but not exclusively in ours. It is strange that those who talk so much about antichrist nowadays never mention this.

To sum up then, antichrists had come in John's day. They were not expected in a remote future time. To be sure, we have those today who oppose the Christ and His teachings. There were (are) many antichrists, not just one great world personality. The antichrists of John's writing were former Christians who had given up the faith, not some mysterious evil force to appear in the twentieth century. Finally, the doctrine of the antichrists was that Jesus did not come in the flesh. Bible teachings about antichrists do not remotely resemble current teachings about such.

Now, what about the mark of the beast? In the Bible, a "mark" could be for identification. (I will come back to that in a moment.) A mark was also used as a blessing to the person marked. For example, it is said in Genesis 4 that Cain killed his brother Abel and God sent him away from his land to "wander" upon the earth. Cain was afraid that anyone he met would kill him. But God insisted that that would not happen, because He, the Lord, would place a mark on Cain that would warn others not to harm him. The act was an act of grace on the part of God. History has misunderstood this mark and often refers to "those with the mark of Cain upon them," meaning a curse. A careful reading of the Bible would avoid that misunderstanding, but some people read little and conclude much. The mark was a sign of God's grace, not a curse.

The Lord's "mark" also meant protection. In Ezekiel chapter 9, God's judgment of disobedient Judah (the reason for which is given in the preceding chapter) would not harm the faithful. These were "marked" on their foreheads so that the judgment would pass by them (Ezekiel 9:6). The Hebrew here describes a well-known mark, namely the alphabetic letter *taw* (or *T*), which was made like an *X*. Some people today sign their names with an *X* from the English alphabet. Job saw himself signing the list of God's charges with his signature or "taw" (Job 31:35).

As with the antichrist, the interpretations of the mark of the beast are numerous. Some of us can remember, prior to and during World War II, the blue eagle symbol of the NRA (National Recovery Act) was interpreted by some as the mark of the beast. In that case, Franklin D. Roosevelt would have been the beast, I suppose. As a child, I can remember hearing preachers making a big deal of that. They were just as certain as their counterparts today that they had found fulfillment of Bible prophecy.

Such guesses have faded from the scene, but new ones crop up regularly. Among some of the more recent ones is the bar code price mark on merchandise in the retail stores, or such as you sometimes see on envelopes required of bulk mail for lower postal rates. It is merely the electronic zip code number. Some people refuse to have a credit card or a social security number containing three sixes for fear it is the mark of the beast.

Well, marks were used in the Bible for a variety of purposes:

(1) They were sometimes signs of God's grace, as in the case of Cain.

(2) A person could affirm or give his oath by signing his mark, or "taw."

(3) A mark could be a sign of God's protection of those marked. And

(4) A mark can designate ownership.

But those who speak of the antichrist as one person representing all that is evil and who is to come in our day, speak of the "mark of the antichrist" in Revelation 13:16. We are told the mark is worn by the followers of antichrist, who is the embodiment of all apostasy. Once more they interpret the figurative language of the book of Revelation literally and see a literal mark placed on the foreheads of antichrist's followers for identification purposes. Again, it is insisted that the marking would be in the distant future, in our time, although we have seen that antichrists were mentioned by John concerning persons in his own day, the first century A.D.

However, the greatest speculation about the mark of the beast is associated with the beast's number—666 (Revelation 13:18). It is hard to give the variety of interpretations that have been given this number, 666. It is said to apply to the antichrist, despite the fact that *antichrist* never appears in the book of Revelation.

Some have said that the number 666 points to Nero Caesar. If we were forced to give an interpretation to some specific person, Nero would be the most likely candidate. If we should decide for Nero, however, we would immediately defeat the premillennial interpretations because Nero lived during John's lifetime. Once again we see that the Bible is not seeing a distant scene near the time of Christ's return.

A favorite theory of some interpreters is a reference to Roman Catholic Church apostasy, the pope being the antichrist. But if this is so, what possible meaning could the passage have for the Christians in Asia Minor in A.D. 95? It would be strange indeed if the Scripture passages addressed to the churches of Asia in John's day had nothing to say to them.

During World War II, the antichrist, his mark and number were occasionally associated with Adolph Hitler. The number once again gives no evidence for such an interpretation, and John's people would be left without a message again.

Well, the number of the beast is the significant thing in Revelation, not the name. The number 6 was the number of humanity, since it was one short of 7, the number for deity or perfection. The great evil of the one described is greatly amplified by using the number three times—666. It is the number of a man and his great evil, but it was never intended to describe remote times in history. To be sure, evil men live in all periods of human history, including our own, but the best evidence points to someone in John's own day, or the first century A.D.

In all the confusion created by premillennial theories, I find myself having greater and greater confidence in the Bible. The Bible does not engage in fantasy or speculation but remains firm and true from generation to generation.

People who follow the premillennial books and preachers who are so captivated by their supposed understanding of "prophetic times" would do well to heed the words of Charles Spurgeon, the eminent nineteenth century Baptist preacher of London. He said:

> So, too, certain persons who are always given to curious speculations need warning. When they read the Bible it is not to find out whether they are saved or no, but to know whether we are under the third or fourth vial, when the millennium is going to be, or what is the battle of Armageddon. Ah, sir, search out all these things if thou hast time and skill, but look to thine own salvation first. The book of Revelation, blessed is he that understands it, but not unless, first of all, he understands this, "He that believeth and is baptized shall be saved."

My friend, I pray you will not become so captivated by the fantasies of modern prophets that you lose sight of the real message of the Bible—that is, the coming of Jesus Christ to die on the cross to make atonement for your sins. The real question is not "Is Saddam Hussein the antichrist?" or the number 666 his number in the foreheads of his followers, but are you a Christian, a child of God, ready to go and be with Christ when He comes for His redeemed? I hope you are; but if you are not, I hope you will come to Christ today. Will you obey Him in baptism and be saved by the blood He shed for you at Calvary (Mark 16:16; Revelation 1:5)? If we may assist you, we would be thrilled.

In churches of Christ, our faith, our preaching, our worship, our mission, our hope are all focused on Jesus Christ, not on some fictitious antichrist you are hearing so much about today. And when you come to worship with us, we will only seek to draw you nearer to Him. God bless you. I love you.

QUESTIONS FOR CLASS DISCUSSION

1. Describe the dispensational-premillennialist antichrist.
2. From the four passages of Scripture that mention antichrist(s), give four differences between biblical antichrist and premillennial antichrist.
3. Who is antichrist?
4. Name some supposed marks of the beast. What are some "marks" not named by the author?
5. What is the significance of the number 6?
6. What is the meaning of the number 666?
7. Where are "antichrist" and "mark of the beast" related in the Scriptures?
8. What is the important message for us?
9. Should preaching be focused on Saddam Hussein or Jesus Christ?

8

Revelation and Coming Events

Revelation 22:18, 19

For I testify unto every man that heareth the words of the prophecy of this book, If any man shall add unto these things, God shall add unto him the plagues that are written in this book: and if any man shall take away from the words of the book of this prophecy, God shall take away his part out of the book of life, and out of the holy city, and from the things which are written in this book.

The book of Revelation is the most confused, abused, and misused book of the Bible. No book of the Scripture has been used as often to frighten people into religion as the book of Revelation. Literally hundreds of books have been published in the last decade declaring what Revelation says about world events in the twentieth century. Many of them have elaborate time tables that give step-by-step predictions of coming events. "The Mark of the Beast," "666," and "Armageddon" are terms from Revelation that are commonly used to scare people into religion.

But does the book of Revelation really and truly predict twentieth century events? Really now, does it speak of the European Common Market? Henry Kissinger? The current struggle between the world's two great super-powers and their allies? What does the book of Revelation itself have to say about itself? To whom was it written? When? Where? For what purpose?

Much of the preaching we are hearing today from the book of Revelation is pure speculation. More often than not, a sensational evangelist takes a passage from Revelation, lifts it from its context, puts it in a twentieth century context, and forces upon it a meaning which it does not have and never did have. Every one of them whom I have heard has woven his own peculiar theory, and in spite of the fact that they all claim to have received their prophecy directly from God through a personal visitation of the Holy Spirit, each one's theory is different from all the others. That seems strange, doesn't it? It seems that if what they are speculating is the real intent of the book of Revelation, they would all be saying the same thing, doesn't it? Some of them would have us believe that Henry Kissinger is the beast of Revelation. Others tell us that the little computer price code on a tube of toothpaste or a magazine or any other piece of merchandise is the "mark of the beast." Others think they see the European Common Market in Revelation, and on and on the list could go.

Two things I know:

(1) The book of Revelation is not a book of confusion and fear, but one of encouragement and hope in the time of trial. And

(2) We are in grave danger of eternal torment if we add to or diminish from the book.

Right at the close of it, the Lord said:

> I testify unto every man that heareth the words of the prophecy of this book, if any man shall add unto these things, God shall add unto him the plagues that are written in this book; and if any man shall take away from the words of the book of this prophecy, God shall take away his part out of the book of life, and out of the holy city, and from the things which are written in this book (Revelation 22:18, 19).

Revelation and Coming Events

Therefore, we do not want to add any thing to it, or take any thing out of it, or change it in any way to make it mean something it does not mean.

What is the book of Revelation all about anyway? Turn with me to the first chapter. Remember now, just as it is with understanding any book of the Bible, we must approach this study with the idea of determining what the author meant for it to mean when he wrote it. Revelation is a first century book and it means today just what it meant then. So the question is not, What do I think the book of Revelation means? but, What did the author mean when he wrote his book? Let us see if we can determine that right now.

First, we learn that John the beloved apostle is the author (Revelation 1:1, 4) and that he is receiving his message as a revelation from Jesus Christ while he (John) is exiled for the cause of Christ on the Isle of Patmos (Revelation 1:1, 9). The authorship of the book is no problem to us.

Next, we learn that the book was written to the seven churches of Asia. Verse 4 just says, "Unto the seven churches which are in Asia; grace be unto you, and peace . . ." And again in verses 10 and 11, John writes:

> I was in the Spirit on the Lord's day, and heard behind me a great voice, as of a trumpet, saying, I am Alpha and Omega, the first and the last; and, What thou seest, write in a book, and send it unto the seven churches which are in Asia (Revelation 1:10, 11).

And then He names them: Ephesus, Smyrna, Pergamos, Thyatira, Sardis, Philadelphia, and Laodicea.

So then, it was not written to twentieth century America about twentieth century politics either in the Middle East or in America. What would the Lord be writing to seven churches of first century Asia about? Would He be telling them about Henry Kissinger? Would He be writing them about the European Common Market or a great conflict between the two great twentieth century super powers and their allies?

Let's see what the book itself says about it. The first verse says, "The revelation of Jesus Christ, which God gave unto Him, to shew unto His servants things which must shortly come to pass." And the third verse says, "Blessed is he that readeth, and they that hear the words of this prophecy, and keep those things which are written therein; for the time is at hand."

Twice in the first three verses of the book, the author declares that the things about which he is writing "must shortly come to pass." And if one should fail to catch that thought, he ends the book the same way. In 22:6 he writes:

> And he said unto me, these things are faithful and true [they are dependable and true, in other words] and the Lord God of the holy prophets sent his angel to shew unto his servants the things which must shortly be done.

And in verse 10 he continues, "He saith unto me, seal not the sayings of the prophecy of this book; for the time is at hand." In other words, do not seal up the book because these events will transpire very soon. Compare that with what He told Daniel about his prophecy in Daniel 8:26 and 12:4, to seal up the book because the fulfillment would be "after many days." So whatever John is writing to the seven churches of Asia about is not something about twentieth century world politics, but something about which they would be concerned very shortly in their very own lifetime.

What is John writing those first century Christians about that must shortly come to pass? Revelation was written to people who were being severely persecuted by Rome! The severity of their persecution defies a description. They were in great agony, both emotionally and physically. They had refused to worship the emperor and they were being punished unmercifully for it and, of course, their faith was being sorely tested. To the church in Smyrna, John wrote:

> I know thy works and tribulation, and poverty (but thou art rich) and I know the blasphemy of them which say they are Jews, and are not, but are the synagogue of

Satan. Fear none of those things which thou shalt suffer; behold the devil shall cast some of you into prison, that ye may be tried; and ye shall have tribulation ten days (Revelation 2:9, 10).

And in 6:9 he writes:

When He had opened the fifth seal, I saw under the altar the souls of them that were slain for the word of God, and for the testimony which they held; and they cried with a loud voice, saying, how long, oh Lord, holy and true, dost thou not judge and avenge our blood on them that dwell on the earth?

Physical, emotional, spiritual agonies are described in these verses! How could they possibly endure much longer? Well, the book of Revelation was written them to give them courage, to build their faith, and to enhance their hope. It is a message of victory in Jesus Christ! It says over and over and over again:

To him that overcometh will I give to eat of the tree of life, which is in the midst of the paradise of God (2:7).

Be thou faithful unto death, and I will give thee a crown of life (2:10).

He that overcometh shall not be hurt of the second death (2:11).

To him that overcometh will I give to eat of the hidden manna (2:17).

He that overcometh, the same shall be clothed in white raiment; and I will not blot out his name out of the book of ife, but I will confess his name before my Father, and before his angels (3:5).

Don't you see that the message of Revelation is not about world politics two thousand years removed from those persecuted saints? Of what interest would those things be to suffering disciples of Jesus Christ of the first century? It was a specific message for a specific people in a specific time for a specific purpose. Its theme can easily be summed up in chapter 17, verse 14:

> These shall make war with the Lamb, and the Lamb shall overcome them; for he is Lord of lords, and King of kings; and they that are with him are called, and chosen and faithful.

I love that! He is saying they may kill you and destroy you, but you will win because you are with the Lord, and He is Lord of lords and King of kings; and because He is, and you are His, you will win!! The victory is yours! Do not give up!!

My friend, the book of Revelation means today just what it meant then. It is a book of faith and courage and hope and victory over all your enemies in Christ Jesus. Do not be frightened or deceived by false teachers who come around with their own specially woven mysterious, speculative theories about certain supposed future political events as though they are sustained by the book of Revelation.

But why is the book of Revelation so difficult to read and so hard to understand? Why are there so many graphic pictures? The word *revelation* comes from the Greek word *apocalypse* which means "an uncovering, or a revealing." That seems kind of strange to us because in our generation it seems to be anything but that. It is a very difficult book to understand. It is a type of literature that was used by the Hebrews for hundreds of years before Revelation. It is a type of literature in which the theme is developed by using signs and symbols.

So if you had been a Jew, familiar with Old Testament apocalyptic literature, you would have known the meanings of the symbols. But if you had been a Roman and unfamiliar with Hebrew scripture, you would not have known what Revelation was all about. Or if you were wanting to send a secret message to somebody who understood the symbols and you wanted to conceal the message from their enemies who did not understand the symbols, you would write to them in apocalyptic style, signs and symbols. That is what the Lord did in Revelation. And that is what the book declares at the very outset.

> The revelation of Jesus Christ, which God gave unto him, to shew unto his servants things which must shortly

come to pass; and he sent and signified it by his angel unto his servant John (Revelation 1:1).

He communicated it to John by signs. He *signified* it to him. It was somewhat like a secret code during war time. The Christians, because they understood the symbols, would understand the message, but any Roman authority who might come into possession of the book would not.

Apocalyptic books were generally written in hard, hard times for the Jews. They were written to prophecy hope and encouragement and God's judgment on those who are evil. And that is what the book of Revelation is really all about, not about a bunch of utter nonsense about twentieth century world conditions and politics.

If you were a prisoner for your faith in Christ, in jail in Ephesus, and John wrote you a book telling you all about twentieth century politics, how much good and comfort and encouragement to keep the faith would that be to you?

Revelation continues to encourage the Christian to overcome, to be faithful unto death so as to receive the victory crown, the crown of life. Say, my friend, are you a Christian? If you are not, I want to take just a moment to encourage you to confess Christ here in this life so He can confess you before the Father in heaven (Matthew 10:32, 33); to turn your life around in repentance (Acts 17:30) and live it for God; and to be baptized into Jesus Christ, into His death, and be washed in the blood of the Lamb of God and begin your heavenward journey today (Romans 6:3, 4). If you are a church member who has not been faithful, and overcome, oh, how important it is for you to reverse your direction and come back to God. Will you? God bless you. I really do love you.

QUESTIONS FOR CLASS DISCUSSION

1. What is the book of Revelation about?
2. Who wrote it?
3. To whom was it written?
4. What interest would revelations of twentieth century world events be for the people to whom the book was originally written? Explain.
5. Why is Revelation so difficult to read and understand?
6. How do some people use a present day fulfillment of Revelation in preaching?

9

Understanding Revelation

Revelation 1:1-3

The Revelation of Jesus Christ, which God gave unto him, to shew unto his servants things which must shortly come to pass; and he sent and signified it by his angel unto his servant John: who bare record of the word of God, and of the testimony of Jesus Christ, and of all things that he saw. Blessed is he that readeth, and they that hear the words of this prophecy, and keep those things which are written therein: for the time is at hand.

Operation Desert Storm weighs heavily on all our minds, especially those who have loved ones directly engaged in the conflict. In every world crisis, self-styled prophets appear in great numbers to explain how those events fulfill Bible prophecy, are a "count-down to Armageddon," and are "signs of Christ's coming" and the "end of the world." Because of the geographical location of this conflict, and because it is understood by many to be an attack on Israel, these prophets are very vocal right now.

Much of this speculation is based on private interpretations of the book of Revelation. I say private interpretations because if you are listening to more than one of them, you must know that despite all their claims to direct revelations from God, each one has his (or her) own unique version, and what follows is accurately described by Hap Cawood of the Cox News Service as "nonsense," but what I will more gracefully call "confusion."

I hope I am not adding to that confusion by this study and probably would not have anything to say about it at all except that so very many of our television audience from coast to coast are asking for some help out of the chaotic situation.

I know of no piece of literature in existence that is as widely misunderstood and badly mutilated as the last book of the Bible called Revelation. The Holy Spirit surely knew it would be so, for He closed the book with a very solemn warning which applies to all the Scriptures, but especially to Revelation. He cautioned:

> I testify unto every man that heareth the words of the prophecy of this book, If any man shall add unto these things, God shall add unto him the plagues that are written in this book: and if any man shall take away from the words of the book of this prophecy, God shall take away his part out of the book of life, and out of the holy city, and from the things which are written in this book.

My friend, it is a solemn thing to tamper with God's word, to make it suit a fancy or fallacy of our own liking. Let's begin by reading the first three verses of the book:

> The Revelation of Jesus Christ, which God gave unto him, to shew unto his servants things which must shortly come to pass; and he sent and signified it by his angel unto his servant John: who bare record of the word of God, and of the testimony of Jesus Christ, and of all things that he saw. Blessed is he that readeth, and they that hear the words of this prophecy, and keep those things which are written therein: for the time is at hand (Revelation 1:1-3).

Can we understand Revelation? Perhaps you have heard it said that God never intended for us to understand this book. Or perhaps you have heard the opposite: "Revelation is easily understood." Both statements are incorrect. In verse 3 of the passage we just read, John said that the person who *reads* and *hears* and *keeps* the things written therein *will receive a blessing*. But it is not easy. It requires serious study. With a desire to be helpful, I am suggesting some very basic rules to apply in such a study.

First, whether it is Revelation or I Thessalonians, the reader must *determine the purpose of the book*. Dr. Bill Jones of the Bible Department of Oklahoma Christian University tells about three young men, studying to be preachers, who spent their noon hours at a local high school gym keeping in shape by playing a little basketball. The janitor who let them in each noon would sit in the stands and read his Bible while they played. One young man became curious and asked the janitor what he was reading. The answer was, "The book of Revelation." Having done some study in this unusual book himself, the young man grinned and asked him, "Do you understand what it's saying?" The janitor didn't hesitate a moment in giving a yes answer. "You do? Well, what does it mean?" Looking up from his Bible, the man answered, "It means that Jesus is going to win."

This man had studied the book carefully. You cannot give a better statement of the purpose of the book of Revelation than that. Revelation deals with the struggle of the church against the Roman Empire in which Christ and His disciples were going to win! The historical events discussed in it have been fulfilled, yet it contains precious and eternal truths for our comfort and encouragement in our conflict with evil in our present generation.

Next, the book must be interpreted *in its own time frame*. The very first sentence of the book says, "The Revelation of Jesus Christ, which God gave unto him, to shew unto his servants things which *must shortly come to pass*." And verse 3 says: "*The time is at hand.*" And near the end it says it again in 22:6: "The Lord God of the holy prophets sent his angel to shew unto his servants *the things which must shortly be done*." And once more before the close, in 22:10: "Seal not the sayings of the prophecy of this book: *for the time is at hand*." Any understanding of the book that disregards these plain and repeated declarations is a misunderstanding.

The third rule is also found in verse 1: "And he sent and *signified it* by his angel unto John." Much of the language of Revelation is symbolism—signs and symbols, sometimes called "apocalyptic" language. The general rule in studying Scripture, such as the writings of Paul or Peter, is to understand it literally unless you are forced by context to interpret it figuratively. In an apocalyptic book such as Revelation, the reader should interpret it symbolically unless he is forced by context to interpret it literally.

The common error is to symbolize parts of Revelation when the need is not there and to ignore the symbolism in passages that demand it. The explanation that says "fire and brimstone" are nuclear explosions; "locusts" are Cobra helicopters; and "swords and shields" are tanks and missiles is *fabrication*, not *interpretation*, and is too far-fetched to merit consideration by the serious Bible student.

The fourth principle I will suggest is to *look at the book in its entirety*. Do not try to interpret a verse or two here or there, independently. You are looking at the entire picture, not a single piece of a jigsaw puzzle or one piece of a mosaic.

Now, with these principles in mind, let us take a look at the book itself. Upon reading it through, we notice that it easily falls into three divisions. The major line of division is between chapters 11 and 12. Chapters 1 to 11 warn the churches of Asia to expect persecution and assures them that their Lord knows their struggles and will give them strength to endure.

The second division, chapters 12 to 20, asks the question, "*Why* is the church being persecuted?" The answer is that the beast from the land, the beast from the sea, and the great harlot are inspired in their evil ways by the devil or Satan (12:9). But Christians are promised that their enemies will not win, but that in the end Christ and His church will be victorious over the devil and his allies. That promise is for us as well as the first century church.

Understanding Revelation

The third division, of course, consists of the last two chapters which reveal the rewards for the victors. That is a quick overview. Now let us look in a little more detail at the first division.

In chapters 1 to 3, Jesus speaks to the seven churches of Asia. John, the apostle, who is their brother and companion in tribulation, has been exiled on the isle of Patmos "for the word of God and the testimony of Jesus Christ" (1:9). He yearns to know how things are going with the beloved churches he knew so well. He knows they, too, are being persecuted by Rome and he hopes to be encouraged by a word from them.

In the first chapter the Lord appears to John in radiance. When John sees Him, he falls at His feet as dead! Jesus reminds him that He is alive and has the power to rescue the saints. In chapters 2 and 3, Jesus both comforts and warns the seven churches of Asia. He speaks of the good and the bad in these churches. Some interpreters insist that these are not literal churches, but they symbolize seven periods of history, that we are now living in the Laodicean Age, named for the last church Jesus discussed, and for that reason the Lord will come again in our lifetime. But this is one of those instances to which we referred a moment ago when we said some interpret symbolically when the text does not demand it. There is too much evidence that these were literal churches, unrelated to questionable historical periods that supposedly reach into the twentieth century.

In chapters 4 and 5, we read of the Victorious Lamb and the Sealed Book. John is invited into heaven where he is permitted to see God on His throne. The message is "God reigns!" and He has not forgotten His people. And He is worshiped in the song, "Worthy Art Thou."

Then John sees a book (scroll) in God's right hand. It contains the future fortunes of the churches, but it is tightly sealed, and while it remains sealed, John cannot know that future. The call goes out across heaven, "Who is worthy to open the scroll and break its seals?" John weeps that no one is found worthy to open the seals but is comforted when he sees the Lamb, who is the Son of God, who is worthy and once more the song echoes throughout heaven, "Worthy is the Lamb."

In chapters 11 through 19, the Lamb opens the seals. There are seven seals, the opening of the last of which introduces the sounding of seven trumpets, and at the sounding of the seventh trumpet there are seven bowls or vials. (Seven is the number for perfection.) The first four seals describe the church's struggle. Christ and His people go forth preaching the word and conquering evil—the white horse (6:1, 2)—and are met with conflict, bloodshed, war—the red horse (6:3, 4). They also experience famine due to persecution—the black horse (6:5, 6)—followed by the pale horse of death and pestilence (6:7, 8).

In seals five and six (6:9-11; 12-17), martyred saints pray for God's aid and divine judgment follows. But in it all, Jesus is the Overcomer! The Victor! The six trumpets (8:6 - 9:21) sound further judgments on those who persecute Christians. They remind us of the plagues that came upon Egypt and are for the same purpose: to afford the persecutor the opportunity to repent, but in both cases he only hardens his heart. Chapters 10 and 11 are real comfort to the oppressed people of God.

Chapters 12 through 20 assure Christians that any and all efforts by the devil and his allies:

(1) the beast from the sea representing the Roman Empire of John's day,

(2) the beast of the earth who symbolizes the false religion (emperor worship), and

(3) the great harlot, representing the evil city of Rome itself,

will be defeated. Then the Lord will be the Victor!—along with His church. Their reward is described in chapters 20 through 22.

Well, we have had to hurry, but by now you can see that the overview of the book of Revelation is not all that difficult. The message is plain. But what about those who say they are preaching and teaching Revelation, who ignore the overview?

Well, obviously they are not seeing any single text in its context and the inevitable result is an erroneous conclusion and false teaching.

For example, chapter 20 is often interpreted, without respect for the overview, to mean that Jesus will return to earth to reign in Jerusalem for a period of one thousand years. The total interpretation assumes a message for *our* time, but *none* for the people who suffered in John's day. Does it not seem strange that the book, written to give comfort and encouragement to the beleaguered saints of the first century A.D., are given no message at this crucial point? Such an interpretation violates the total purpose and picture of the book we have just surveyed, since it offers no help at all to John and his fellow Christians. It also disregards John's repeated statements that the things he is writing about must "shortly come to pass."

Well, whatever else we may learn from Revelation, we have certainly learned the importance of being a faithful child of God, of having one's name written in the Lamb's Book of Life. Is yours, my friend? Do not permit the prophets of peril with their "signs" of Christ's coming, a great battle of Armageddon, and the end of the world, turn your attention from the important thing—being born anew into the family of God at once. Be ready when He comes, whenever that time is, and all will be well with your soul. God bless you. Really now, I love you.

Chapter 9

QUESTIONS FOR CLASS DISCUSSION

1. Explain God's punishment upon those who add to or diminish from the book of Revelation. Does the same apply to *all* of God's revelation? To the Old Testament and the New Testament?
2. Show the harmony of God's prophets and preachers in the Scriptures. How do you account for it? If different "prophets" today are being led by the same Spirit, would they not likewise speak harmoniously? What, then, does this say about modern prophets?
3. Discuss at least four suggested rules for understanding the book of Revelation.
4. Give the three divisions in the "overview" of the book and what each does for the complete revelation.
5. How would you sum up in one sentence the message of Revelation?
6. After surveying the book, what would you say we should certainly learn from it?

10

Matthew 24

Mattthew 24:1-3

And Jesus went out, and departed from the temple: and his disciples came to him for to shew him the buildings of the temple. And Jesus said unto them, See ye not all these things? verily I say unto you, There shall not be left here one stone upon another, that shall not be thrown down. And as he sat upon the mount of Olives, the disciples came unto him privately, saying, Tell us, when shall these things be? and what shall be the sign of thy coming, and of the end of the world?

For generations now, when there is an international crisis or military conflict or a famine or an earthquake of any magnitude anywhere in the world, there are those people who see it as a sign of the imminent return of Christ and the end of the world. It probably goes without saying that the Scripture most often used to corroborate that idea is the twenty-fourth chapter of Matthew because it speaks of such cataclysmic events. If the Lord intended for the things of which He spoke in this passage to be used as "signs" of His coming, then it is important to all of us to know about it. If, on the other hand, that is not His intent at all, then to use the passage for that purpose constitutes a misrepresentation of Jesus and misuse or abuse of the Scripture. For that reason—not to prove a point or to engage in debate with anyone either way, but for the purpose of trying to learn what Jesus actually wanted us to know—let us examine the passage.

It is necessary to understanding any passage that it be studied in its context or its setting. Failure to follow this common sense rule is the cause of much confusion in the religious world. We just simply cannot take a passage (any passage) out of its setting and wave the Bible around and shout, "There it is; it says it, I believe it, and that settles it." That sounds smart and it will draw an applause from an unthinking crowd; but if we are seeking the truth, we must consider the circumstances under which this chapter was spoken, to whom it was spoken, and, if possible, the intent.

In the preceding chapter, Jesus had repeatedly pronounced woes on the Jews. Seven times He had said, "Woe unto you, scribes and Pharisees, hypocrites." Jerusalem had rejected the prophets and by so doing had rejected Him, their Messiah, for which He pronounced destruction on the city in their very own generation. "O Jerusalem, Jerusalem," He cried:

> Thou that killest the prophets, and stonest them which are sent unto thee, how often would I have gathered thy children together, even as a hen gathereth her chickens under her wings, and ye would not! Behold, your house is left unto you desolate. For I say unto you, Ye shall not see me henceforth, till ye shall say, Blessed is he that cometh in the name of the Lord (Matthew 23:35, 36).

With that He moved outside the temple and His disciples called His attention to the temple buildings as if they sought some word of assurance that it might be spared. No, said Jesus, "Verily I say unto you, There shall not be left here one stone upon another, that shall not be thrown down" (24:2).

With those words freshly etched in their minds, they crossed over the Kidron Valley to the Mount of Olives where they had a wide-angle view of the city and the temple. In the privacy of that moment they asked Him two questions. "Tell us," they said:

Matthew 24

(1) "When shall these things be [that is, the things He had been talking about, the destruction of Jerusalem and the temple]?" and

(2) "What shall be the sign of thy coming, and of the end of the world" (verse 3)?

When I say that, I am painfully aware that some very learned and scholarly men, whose judgments I respect very highly, believe that there is only one question there. And it is not as though I have ignored the strong evidence of that possibility. But because of Jesus' reply, personally, I am persuaded there are two: one concerns the destruction of Jerusalem and the other about the Lord's coming and the end of the world. It seems to me that the biggest reason for believing that the disciples asked but one question is the parallel passages in Mark 13 and Luke 21. But even if it were true, the conclusion need not be changed. Christ very clearly divides His answer into two parts: one concerning the destruction of Jerusalem and the other about His return and the end of the world.

In verses 4 to 34, Jesus answers their first question, the one about the destruction of Jerusalem. He has already said it would be in their own generation (23:36). He begins with the warning, "Take heed that no man deceive you. For many shall come in my name, saying, I am Christ, and shall deceive many." That is an appropriate warning; one that is worth repeating in verse 11 and again in verse 24. "For there shall arise false Christs," He says, "and false prophets, and shall shew great signs and wonders [or great miracles]; insomuch that, if it were possible, they shall deceive the very elect."

Then He lists a number of signs of the impending desolation of their city and the temple. There would be false Christs (verse 5). There would be wars and rumors of wars (verse 6). Nation would rise against nation and kingdom against kingdom (verse 7). There would be famines, pestilences, and earthquakes (verse 7). His disciples (the Christians) would be persecuted, even killed (verse 9). Iniquity would abound, thus the love of many would grow cold (verse 12). The gospel of the kingdom would have been preached to every nation in all the world (verse 14). They would see the abomination of desolation spoken by Daniel the prophet (verse 15).

The prophecy mentioned is found in the ninth chapter of Daniel and it gives a time table. By using days for years, the usual and common way of interpreting prophecy, it brings us to that generation then living. In Luke's account of the same conversation, at the point where Matthew says, "When ye ... see the abomination of desolation, spoken of by Daniel the prophet," he says, "When ye shall see Jerusalem compassed with armies, then know that the desolation thereof is nigh" (Luke 21:20). It is only by interrupting the time table between the sixty-ninth and seventieth years and inserting some two thousand years that premillennialists can use that prophecy today to apply to the return of Christ. And He says, "This generation shall not pass, till all these things be fulfilled" (verse 34).

Please notice that all of these signs were, not in answer to their second question concerning His return, but to their first question about the impending destruction of their city and nation, and they were to occur, and did occur, during that generation. Jerusalem was besieged by the Romans in the summer of A.D. 70 and the temple was destroyed. To apply them to twentieth century occurrences and use them as signs of the return of Christ is to misrepresent and misquote the Lord.

But after giving all those signs, Jesus proceeded to tell them what they should do when they began to happen: "Let him [the disciple] that is in Judea flee into the mountains [verse 16]. Let him that is on the housetop [where it was their custom to retire for rest and devotions] not come down to get anything out of the house. [The delay could be disastrous]" (verse 17). Neither is he that is in the field to run back to the house to get his clothes (verse 18). Women with children would find themselves in even greater danger. The disciples were to pray that their escape would not have to be in the winter or on the Sabbath day when the gates of the city would be closed, preventing their escape.

Now when Jesus was speaking of fleeing and escaping, He could not possibly have been speaking of His return and the end of the world, for that will be a universal event from which there will be no escape. It will be impossible to flee. If it is the "great tribulation" of the premillennial theory, there will be no disciples here to flee anyway because they are supposed to have been snatched already up in the "rapture." Well, these "signs of the times" are obviously not to be applied to the return of Christ and the end of the world but to the destruction of Jerusalem and the State of Israel. Jesus said, "Verily I say unto you, This generation shall not pass, till all these things be fulfilled."

Perhaps you are wondering about verses 29 and 30:

> Immediately after the tribulation of those days shall the sun be darkened, and the moon shall not give her light, and the stars shall fall from heaven, and the powers of the heavens shall be shaken; and then shall appear the sign of the Son of man in heaven; and then shall all the tribes of the earth mourn, and they shall see the Son of man coming in the clouds of heaven with power and great glory.

This is prophetic language used often with reference to great disasters and the fall of nations, powers, and dignitaries. For example, with reference to the fall of Babylon, Isaiah declared, "For the stars of heaven and the constellations thereof shall not give their light; the sun shall be darkened in his going forth, the moon shall not give her light to shine" (Isaiah 13:10). Similar language is used in reference to the destruction of Damascus in Isaiah 17, of Ethiopia in Isaiah 18, and of Egypt in Isaiah 19. They are just as applicable to the cataclysmic end of the Jewish nation as any other.

That all these things discussed to this point are in answer to the first question with regard to the destruction of Jerusalem, there can be no doubt. Verse 34 quotes Jesus as saying, "Verily I say unto you, this generation shall not pass, till all these things be fulfilled." If we cannot believe that, there is no reason to believe any part of the whole chapter.

In verse 35 Jesus responds to the second question: "What shall be the sign of thy coming, and of the end of the world?" "Heaven and earth shall pass away," He tells them, "but my words shall not pass away." Then He adds, "Of that day and hour [the day and hour when heaven and earth shall pass away] knoweth no man, no, not the angels of heaven, but my Father only." He knew about the first event and gave them signs of it, but not of the second. There will be no signs or warnings of Christ's coming and the end of the world. No man on earth knows the day or the hour. Anyone who says he knows is not telling you the truth, or Christ did not tell the truth. It is just that simple.

The remainder of chapter 24 and all of chapter 25 are Jesus' assurances of the sudden, unannounced coming of the Son of man. He says it will be so sudden that of two men in the field, one shall be taken and the other left (verse 40), and of the two women at the mill, one shall be taken and the other left (verse 41). He does not mean that one is taken up in a rapture and the other left to suffer the tribulation, but that some will be ready and some will not. And there will be no time for getting ready.

He uses several illustrations to show that it will be at an unexpected time. First He says, "As the days of Noe [Noah] were, so shall also the coming of the Son of man be" (verse 37). The people of Noah's day were living perfectly normal lives; they were eating and drinking and marrying and giving in marriage right up until the time of the flood. Then He says it will be like a thief in the night (verse 43):

> But if the goodman of the house had known in what watch the thief would come, he would have watched, and would not have suffered his house to be broken up. Therefore be ye also ready: for in such an hour as ye think not the Son of man cometh.

It will be as the unexpected return of the land owner who finds some of his servants faithful, while others, thinking their lord has delayed his coming and there is time enough yet to get things ready, are unfaithful and evil (verses 45-51). His message is "Therefore be ye also ready: for in such an hour as ye think not the Son of man cometh."

In chapter 25, He speaks of ten virgins who had been invited to the marriage. Five of them were wise and five were foolish. The wise were prepared. They had oil in their lamps; but the foolish did not. The bridegroom tarried, tarried until midnight, as a matter of fact. Then suddenly, while they slumbered and slept, the announcement came, "Behold, the bridegroom cometh; go ye out to meet him." But the foolish were not ready. The wise arose and went in and the door was shut. The others were left out.

The important message for us in Matthew 24 is not signs of Christ's coming and the end of the world, for no one knows. Even our Lord said He did not know, nor the angels in heaven, only God Himself. So we will have no signs, no warnings; we will not know the day or the hour when the Son of God comes for His own. It is urgent, then, that we be prepared for it, right now and always.

If you are not a Christian, it is foolish of you not to be. You really should believe in Jesus Christ (John 8:24). Put your trust and hope of salvation in Him. You should get your life turned around today. That is what the Bible calls repentance and God commands all of us to repent (Acts 17:30). You should be joined to Christ in baptism, immersed into His death and washed in His blood, buried with Him and raised from the grave of water to live a new life with Him (Romans 6:3, 4). Do not wait. Remember Jesus said:

> Whosoever heareth these sayings of mine, and doeth them, I will liken him unto a wise man, which built his house upon a rock: and the rain descended, and the floods came, and the winds blew, and beat upon that house; and it fell not: for it was founded upon a rock.

And every one that heareth these sayings of mine, and doeth them not, shall be likened unto a foolish man, which built his house upon the sand: and the rain descended, and the floods came, and the winds blew, and beat upon that house; and it fell: and great was the fall of it.

Do not be foolish. God bless you now, I love you.

QUESTIONS FOR CLASS DISCUSSION

1. How many questions did the disciples ask Jesus in Matthew 24:3? Why do you say so?
2. How did Jesus answer?
3. Name as many signs of the impending disaster as you can.
4. How can we be sure these signs were not of Christ's return?
5. Even if the dispensational-premillennial doctrines are true, why could these signs not be references to Christ's return?
6. To what does Jesus statement, "This generation shall not pass away till all these things be fulfilled," apply?
7. What signs will be given of His coming?
8. What of people who say God has spoken to them and told them when Christ will come?
9. What is important about not knowing the time of our Lord's return?
10. Are you ready for it?

11

The Second Coming of Christ

Hebrews 9:24-28

For Christ is not entered into the holy places made with hands, which are the figures of the true; but into heaven itself, now to appear in the presence of God for us: nor yet that he should offer himself often, as the high priest entereth into the holy place every year with blood of others; for then must he often have suffered since the foundation of the world: but now once in the end of the world hath he appeared to put away sin by the sacrifice of himself. And as it is appointed unto men once to die, but after this the judgment: so Christ was once offered to bear the sins of many; and unto them that look for him shall he appear the second time without sin unto salvation.

When our Lord's personal ministry on the earth was almost completed and the cross was in view where He was soon to finish the work of redemption which the Father had sent Him to do, He announced His impending death and departure to His chosen apostles. Quite naturally, they were saddened and were very sorrowful. Of course they were. In an attempt to comfort them, He made a promise: "I go to prepare a place for you," He said. "And if I go to prepare a place for you, I will come again, and receive you unto myself; that where I am, there ye may be also" (John 14:1, 2).

Lest any of us should forget that promise, Jesus instituted the Lord's supper. In the first letter to the church in Corinth, the Holy Spirit said:

> He took bread: and when he had given thanks, he broke it, and said, Take, eat: this is my body, which is broken for you: this do in remembrance of me. After the same manner also he took the cup, when he had supped, saying, This cup is the new testament in my blood: this do ye, as oft as ye drink it, in remembrance of me. For as often as you eat this bread, and drink this cup, ye do shew [proclaim] the Lord's death till he come (I Corinthians 11:22-26).

Luke the inspired historian says that the first century disciples, under the leadership of the Holy Spirit, came together upon the first day of the week to observe this memorial in anticipation of His return (Acts 20:7). And it is on the strength of that promise, "I will come again," that His disciples continue, almost twenty centuries later, to eat the bread and drink the cup on the first day of every week. You will find it so in churches of Christ everywhere. When you think of it, the continuance of the Lord's supper in the present day congregation borders on the miraculous and is one of the most convincing verifications we have, despite some modern teaching that He has already returned, that Jesus will some day "appear the second time," not to bear our sins as He once did on the cross, but to consummate our salvation. What a great promise! Confirmed or sealed with the Lord's supper!

Thus, one of the cardinal doctrines of Christianity is the second coming of Christ and there are literally scores of references to it in the Scriptures. Christians live in joyous anticipation of the time when He shall come to receive His own. In other words, the Christian says, "The Lord said it; that settles it; I believe it."

But there are two extreme views about His return: one is skepticism, the other is speculation. One doubts it will ever happen and the other weaves all kinds of fantasies about it, even to setting dates for it.

Concerning the skeptics, the apostle Peter warned:

> There shall come in the last days scoffers, walking after their own lusts, and saying, Where is the promise of his

coming? for since the fathers fell asleep, all things continue as they were from the beginning of the creation. For this they willingly are ignorant of, that by the word of God the heavens were of old, and the earth standing out of the water and in the water: whereby the world that then was, being overflowed with water, perished: but the heavens and the earth, which are now, by the same word are kept in store, reserved unto fire against the day of judgment and perdition of ungodly men.

But beloved be not ignorant of this one thing, that one day is with the Lord as a thousand years, and a thousand years as one day. The Lord is not slack concerning his promise, as some men count slackness; but is longsuffering to us-ward, not willing that any should perish, but that all should come to repentance. But the day of the Lord will come as a thief in the night: in the which the heavens shall pass away with a great noise, and the elements shall melt with fervent heat, the earth also and the works that are therein shall be burned up (II Peter 3:3-10).

There are six things to remember from that reading:

(1) It is a mistake to grow skeptical and faithless simply because our Lord has delayed His coming and the world just keeps "goin' along" as it always has.

(2) You have to remember that time is not as important to the eternal God as it is to us. The psalmist prayed, "A thousand years in thy sight are but as yesterday when it is past, and as a watch in the night" (Psalm 90:4). Applying that truth to this situation, Peter reminds us that with God a thousand years is as a day and a day is as a thousand years.

(3) When the Lord makes a promise, you can bank on it. Christ said, "I will come again," so you can be sure of it.

(4) God is being longsuffering toward sinful man because it is not His will that a single one of us should perish; it is

His will that each of us come to repentance. His delay is giving us time to repent.

(5) His coming will be as unannounced and unexpected as a thief in the night. And

(6) His coming will mark the end of this world and everything in it.

I suppose we should not be too surprised that a world whose accomplishments have been as varied and of the magnitude of ours would renounce faith in the unseen realities of the Spirit, to walk by sight. After all, we have launched our rockets to outer space to study the most distant planets of our solar system and come to a better understanding of the world in which we live. We have even made human footprints on the moon and, despite all our problems, we are enjoying a better standard of living than man has ever known.

But it is a disappointment when "the church" becomes so impacted with modern materialism and secularism that it abandons the fundamental doctrines of the New Testament and walks by sight and not by faith. Well, no one who is the least bit familiar with current religious thought and church life would deny that it has happened, not only in teaching, but in practice and, without doubt, it is at least a part of the cause of mediocrity into which the modern church has slipped.

Nor can we deny the other extreme: speculation. It has literally filled the airways and countless numbers of books have been written with every conceivable kind of theory about signs of His coming, a countdown to final things, and every imaginable (and some unimaginable) "prophecy."

But there are some things we can know because of what the Bible says. We can know, for example, that when Jesus comes there will be a general resurrection of the dead. The Christians in Thessalonica were troubled about whether the dead would be at a disadvantage when Jesus comes, whether it would not be better to be living when He comes. Paul wrote them saying:

The Second Coming of Christ

> I would not have you to be ignorant, brethren concerning them which are asleep, that ye sorrow not, even as others which have no hope. For if we believe that Jesus died and rose again, even so them also which sleep in Jesus will God bring with him. For this we say unto by the word of the Lord, that we which are alive and remain unto the coming of the Lord shall not prevent [precede] them which are asleep. For the Lord himself shall descend from heaven with a shout, with the voice of the archangel, and with the trump of God: and the dead in Christ shall rise first. Then we which are alive and remain shall be caught up together with them in the clouds, to meet the Lord in the air: and so shall we ever be with the Lord (I Thessalonians 4:12-17).

While this is a very rapturous occasion, it is not the rapture you hear so much about in modern preaching. It is not a hushed appearance of the Savior in which He quietly steals the saints away and leaves the sinner in great tribulation. As a matter of fact, you will not find that taught in the Scriptures at all.

In the apostle Paul's masterful resurrection sermon in I Corinthians 15, he says:

> Flesh and blood cannot inherit the kingdom of God: neither doth corruption inherit incorruption. Behold, I shew you a mystery, we shall not all sleep [meaning, we will not all be dead], but we shall all be changed, in a moment, in the twinkling of an eye, at the last trump: for the trumpet shall sound, and the dead shall be raised incorruptible, and we shall all be changed. For this corruptible must put on incorruption, and this mortal must put on immortality. So when this corruptible shall have put on incorruption, and this mortal shall have put on immortality, then shall be brought to pass the saying that is written, Death is swallowed up in victory. O death, where is thy sting? O grave where is thy victory? The sting of death is sin; and the strength of sin is the law. But thanks be to God, which giveth us the victory through our Lord Jesus Christ (I Corinthians 15:50-57).

Chapter 11

The Lord teaches the simultaneous resurrection of the good and the bad. He said:

> As the Father hath life in himself; so also hath he given to the Son to have life in himself; and hath given him authority to execute judgment also, because he is the Son of man. Marvel not at this: for the hour is coming, in the which all that are in the graves shall hear his voice, and shall come forth, they that have done good, unto the resurrection of life; and they that have done evil, unto the resurrection of damnation (John 5:26-29).

From that we can also know that at the appearing of our Lord and Savior Jesus Christ, there will be a judgment of the good and the evil.

There is something about His coming we cannot learn from the Scriptures: the time of the event, when it will be. The Scripture we read a moment ago from Peter said, "The day of the Lord will come as a thief in the night"—unannounced—no signs—no countdown, my friend. There will be no signs of His coming. Jesus Himself declared, "Of that day and that hour knoweth no man, no, not the angels which are in heaven, neither the Son, but the Father" (Luke 14:32).

So the word is "watch." In language too clear to be misunderstood, Jesus said:

> Take heed, watch and pray: for ye know not when the time is, for the Son of man is as a man taking a far journey, who left his house, and gave authority to his servants, and to every man his work, and commanded the porter to watch. Watch ye therefore: for ye know not when the master of the house cometh, at even, or at midnight, or at the cock crowing, or in the morning: lest coming suddenly he find you sleeping. And what I say unto you I say unto all, Watch (Mark 13:33-37).

Well, we have learned that Jesus Christ promised He would come again. We have seen that He is not slack (loose) about this promise. We have read that when He comes there will be a resurrection of the dead followed by a judgment of the righteous and the wicked. We have also learned from the word of God that no one knows when He will come, not even the angels, so the key word is "watch" and be ready.

In the parable of the virgins, Jesus taught that His coming will not be the time for preparations. Our text today says that when He comes the second time, He will come, not as Savior, but as Judge of the world.

My friend, are you ready for the coming of the Lord? He might not come for another thousand years or more. But He might come before you complete the reading of this message. It could be in your lifetime or mine. But whether we are living or dead, when Jesus comes, we will be summoned to the bar of divine judgment to give account of our stewardship of life. A faithful steward knows the importance of faith in Christ, as stated simply and marvelously by the Master Himself: " . . . He that believeth on me, though he die, yet shall he live: and whosoever liveth and believeth on me shall never die" (John 11:25, 26).

If we really do believe in Jesus, we believe in His resurrection, His second coming and judgment; for it was Jesus Himself who said:

> He that believeth on me, believeth not on me, but on him that sent me. . . . He that rejecteth me, and receiveth not my words, hath one that judgeth him: the word that I have spoken, the same shall judge him in the last day (John 12:44, 46).

But belief alone is not enough; for in another place the Lord says, "Not every one that saith unto me, Lord, Lord, shall enter into the kingdom of heaven; but he that doeth the will of my Father who is in heaven" (Matthew 7:21).

It is certain that we are not saved by works, and it is equally as certain that we are not saved by faith alone (James 2:24). In the last analysis, it is the blood of Christ that saves (Revelation 1:5) when we are immersed into His death (Romans 6:3, 4).

If you are not in a saved condition today, my friend, I beg of you to prepare for the coming of the Lord at once—today.

Recently, we had a letter from a viewer who said:

> Christ said to His disciples, 'Teach them and baptize them in the name of the Father, Son and Holy Ghost.' I'd like to be baptized so I'd like to talk with a minister here. You said to let you know so I did.

And we responded promptly. I pray you will be as prompt. May God bless you with the courage to do it. I love you.

QUESTIONS FOR CLASS DISCUSSION

1. What great promise did Jesus make to His disciples when He announced His departure?
2. How does the observance of the Lord's supper confirm this promise?
3. What two radical attitudes prevail about the return of Christ?
4. What three things can a person be sure of from reading I Thessalonians 4:12-17?
5. What is the victory mentioned in I Corinthians 15:50-58?
6. Name six things we can know from II Peter 3:3-10.
7. Where is it recorded in the Scriptures that Jesus taught a simultaneous resurrection of the good and the evil?
8. What is there about Christ's coming that we cannot learn from the Bible?
9. Are you a Christian? Why?

12

The Thousand Years of Revelation 20

Revelation 20:1-8

And I saw an angel come down from heaven, having the key of the bottomless pit and a great chain in his hand. And he laid hold on the dragon, that old serpent, which is the devil, and Satan, and bound him a thousand years, and cast him into the bottomless pit, and shut him up, and set a seal upon him, that he should deceive the nations no more, till the thousand years should be fulfilled: and after that he must be loosed a little season.

And I saw thrones, and they sat upon them, and judgment was given unto them: and I saw the souls of them that were beheaded for the witness of Jesus, and for the word of God, and which had not worshipped the beast, neither his image, neither had received his mark upon their foreheads, or in their hands; and they lived and reigned with Christ a thousand years. But the rest of the dead lived not again until the thousand years were finished. This is the first resurrection. Blessed and holy is he that hath part in the first resurrection: on such the second death hath no power, but they shall be priests of God and of Christ, and shall reign with him a thousand years.

And when the thousand years are expired, Satan shall be loosed out of his prison, and shall go out to deceive the nations which are in the four quarters of the earth, Gog, and Magog, to gather them together to battle: the number of whom is as the sand of the sea.

A few days ago I came upon an ad on the church page of our newspaper that said, "Find it in the Bible Yourself. The Mid East in Bible Prophecy. Kingdom Seekers Class."

Talk of Bible prophecy relating to the Middle East subsided following the collapse of the Soviet Union and after the sudden end of the Gulf War. So many "prophecies" and interpretations of prophecies proved to be false that the self-styled prophets are having to go scrambling back to "the drawing board," as it were, to dream up some new fantasies. But from all indications, as we come nearer to the end of the twentieth century and approach the beginning of the twenty-first, there is going to be more and more said about it.

Those who have made an in-depth study of the subject tell us that there is a revival of the doctrine of the immediate return of Christ at the beginning of every new century and we may anticipate an unusual amount of it this time for several reasons.

First, because the twenty-first century ushers in a new millennium. The very vocal premillennial dispensationalists believe that since God created the world in six days and rested on the seventh and because Peter said that one day is as a thousand years with the Lord, using Ussher's chronology, the new millennium will be the seventh after creation—thus sometime around the beginning of the new century the Lord will return and set up His kingdom and reign upon the throne of David in the city of Jerusalem for a thousand years. The idea is that the millennium 2000 is to be that millennium.

Pre means "before" and *millennium* means a "thousand" so *pre-millennial* just means "before a thousand" and in relation to religion it means the return of Jesus *before* the establishment of His thousand-year utopian reign on the earth. There are also *post-millennialists*, meaning they believe Christ will come after a period of great prosperity for the church. *Amillennialists* do not believe the Bible promises a utopia on earth, or that Christ will ever reign in an *earthly* kingdom of any duration, before or after His coming. So millennialism is a doctrine which focuses primarily on the establishment of Christ's kingdom and His universal reign as King of kings and Lord of lords. Today we are looking at the one passage in all the Bible that is at the very heart of premillennial teaching.

As we approach it for meaning, we must remember what we have said in other studies of the book of Revelation: first, this

The Thousand Years of Revelation 20 91

is a book of signs and symbols. This is apocalyptic language and is not to be interpreted literally. The very opening sentence in the book says:

> The Revelation of Jesus Christ, which God gave unto him, to shew unto his servants things which must shortly come to pass; and he sent and *signified* it by his angel unto his servant John.

Second, we must also remember that any passage must be interpreted in its context. To lift a passage out of what comes before and after it, to interpret it any other way than in harmony with the message and purpose of the entire book in which it appears, to make it mean something the author never intended it to mean when it was written is a gross perversion of Scripture. The apostle Peter speaks of those who so "wrest" (twist) the Scriptures as being unlearned and unstable and they do such to their own destruction (II Peter 3:16). So you and I do not want to do that, do we now?

The third principle of biblical interpretation we must observe with this passage (as with all others) is that controversial and difficult passages must always be interpreted in harmony with all plain and simple teachings elsewhere. God never contradicts Himself.

Now, John was exiled on Patmos "for the word of God and for the testimony of Jesus Christ" (Revelation 1:9)—that is, for preaching Christ. He knew the disciples in the area of the seven churches (and others) were also suffering intense persecutions. The message which he received of the Lord, which he wrote them in this book, was to:

(1) tell them God was conscious of the intensity of their persecutions, but that things would even get worse;

(2) exhort and encourage them to be faithful unto death, regardless of what comes; and

(3) assure them they would win because of Christ.

Where does this passage fit into that overall message of Revelation? It is the last, of course. It is not hard to figure that out from the very fact it appears toward the end of the book. But it is a promise of victory. In apocalyptic language, those of them who endure will live and reign with Christ a thousand years. The question is, does this passage teach that Christ is coming back to the earth, set up a kingdom of peace and prosperity, and reign from Jerusalem for a thousand years? Well, let's see.

Verse 1 says, "I saw an angel come down from heaven, having the key of the bottomless pit and a great chain in his hand." Note the symbolism: (1) a key, (2) a chain, (3) a bottomless pit.

Verse 2 says, "And laid hold on the dragon, that old serpent, which is the devil, and Satan, and bound him a thousand years." More symbols: (1) the dragon, (2) the old serpent, (3) a binding of Satan—the implication is with the symbolic chain of verse 1—(4) a thousand years.

Now verse 3: "And cast him into the bottomless pit, and shut him up, that he should deceive the nations no more, till the thousand years should be fulfilled: and after that he must be loosed a little season." The symbolism? (1) A casting of Satan into (2) the bottomless pit and (3) a figurative shutting him up till (4) the end of the symbolic thousand years.

Verse 4:

> And I saw thrones, and they sat upon them, and judgment was given unto them: and I saw the souls of them that were beheaded for the witness of Jesus, and for the word of God, which had not worshipped the beast, neither his image, neither had received his mark upon their foreheads, nor in their hand; and they lived and reigned with Christ a thousand years.

The obvious symbols in that verse are: (1) thrones, (2) the beast, (3) marks in their foreheads or hands, and (4) a thousand year reign.

Verse 5 continues: "But the rest of the dead lived not again until the thousand years were finished. This is the first resurrection." There are only two symbols in that short verse: (1) the end of the thousand years and (2) a resurrection.

From just a reading of the passage, we have learned that a thousand year reign of Christ is *symbolic*. It would be the height of absurdity to pick that one thing out of all those symbols and say *it* is literal. The real truth of the matter is, it symbolizes victory for the ones persecuted for Christ. That harmonizes with other verses in Revelation. For example, Revelation 2:7 says, "To him that overcometh will I give to eat of the tree of life, which is in the midst of the paradise of God." Revelation 2:10 says, " . . . Be thou faithful unto death, and I will give thee a crown of life." Revelation 2:11 says, " . . . He that overcometh shall not be hurt of the second death." Others are Revelation 2:17, 26; 3:5, 12, 21.

Please notice what is *not* mentioned that are so vital to the premillennial theory:

(1) Christ's second coming (nothing is said about it in this passage),

(2) establishment of a kingdom,

(3) an earthly kingdom,

(4) Christ sitting on David's throne, or

(5) the Jews' return to Palestine.

It is clear from reading Matthew, Mark, Luke, and John that the purpose of Christ's earthly ministry was first to seek and save the lost (Luke 19:10) and to establish a kingdom over which He would reign as king. So immediately after His baptism of John in the Jordan and His confrontation with Satan, He returned to Galilee and preached in the synagogues the good news of the kingdom that it was "at hand" (Matthew 4:17). When He had preached so in Nazareth and in Capernaum, the people wanted Him to stay there longer. But He refused saying, "I must preach the kingdom of God to other cities also; for therefore am I sent" (Luke 4:43). And He said, " . . . There be some standing here, which shall not taste of death, till they see the kingdom of God" (Luke 9:27).

The establishment of His kingdom was such an obvious part of His ministry that even Pilate asked Him, "Art thou the King of the Jews?" (Matthew 27:11). The question was prompted by the accusation of those who had brought Him there (John 18:28, 40), a charge they knew He would not deny. Jesus' answer was simply, "Thou sayest," meaning "Yea, it is so."

Jesus then went to the cross. He was crucified, buried, raised from the dead, then appeared to His chosen apostles and said, "All power [authority] hath been given unto me in heaven and in earth" (Matthew 28:18). Can you tell me how much more power Jesus would have if, indeed, He should come again and establish some kind of universal earthly reign? It is just a thought.

Premillennialism says that in order to fulfill the prophecies, Christ will return to earth to be seated on the literal throne of David in Jerusalem. Truly, Isaiah says:

> For unto us a child is born, unto us a son is given: and the government shall be upon his shoulder: and his name shall be called Wonderful, Counsellor, The mighty God, The everlasting Father, The Prince of Peace. Of the increase of his government and peace there shall be no end, upon the throne of David, and upon his kingdom, to order it, and to establish it with judgment and with justice from henceforth even for ever (Isaiah 9:6, 7).

But on the day of Pentecost, Peter preached that Christ had fulfilled those prophecies. Being inspired of the Holy Spirit, he said:

> Men and brethren, let me freely speak unto you of the patriarch David, that he is both dead and buried and his sepulchre is with us unto this day. Therefore being a prophet, and knowing that God had sworn with an oath to him, that of the fruit of his loins, according to the flesh, he would raise up Christ *to sit* [Christ was raised up for this purpose—to sit] on his [David's] throne; he seeing this before spake of the resurrection of Christ, that his soul was not left in [hades], neither his flesh did see corruption. This Jesus hath God raised up, whereof we all are witnesses. Therefore being by the right hand of God exalted, and having received of the Father the promise of the Holy Ghost, he hath shed forth this which

ye now see and hear. For David is not ascended into the heavens: but he saith himself, The Lord said unto my Lord, Sit thou on my right hand, until I make thy foes thy footstool. Therefore let all the house of Israel know assuredly, that God hath made that same Jesus, whom ye have crucified, both Lord and Christ (Acts 2:29-36).

When a New Testament writer or preacher says an Old Testament prophecy is fulfilled, it is fulfilled, my friend. So Christ has already fulfilled those prophecies. Now, as we speak, He sits on the throne of David ruling over His universal kingdom of which there is no end.

First Corinthians 15:22-24 says of the resurrection of the dead:

> As in Adam all die, even so in Christ shall all be made alive. But every man in his own order: Christ the firstfruits; afterward they that are Christ's at his coming. Then cometh the end, when he shall have delivered up the kingdom to God, even the Father. . . .

So Christ's coming will mark the end of the world, and the kingdom over which He now reigns as King of kings and Lord of lords will be ushered into the eternal, glorious state.

The most serious of all the questions posed in this study, then, is citizenship in the kingdom of Christ when He comes. The apostle Paul wrote the church at Colossae that when they became children of God, they were "delivered from the power of darkness, and translated into the kingdom of his dear Son" (Colossians 1:13). And John says he, too, was in the kingdom when he received the revelation and wrote it to the churches of Asia (Revelation 1:9).

My friend, are you a Christian? If you have really accepted Christ as Lord, then that is what He is. If you have not accepted Him, I pray you will confess Him so today. And turning from your sins in repentance, will you then arise and be baptized into His death and wash away your sins in His precious blood (Acts 22:16; Revelation 1:5)? If I may assist you, please call on me.

We mentioned one of the basic rules of biblical interpretation is to interpret the passage under consideration in the light of its context, the verses before it and after it. In light of that, it is interesting to observe that every time the kingdom is mentioned in the book of Revelation, a first century document, it is mentioned as presently in existence. For example, Revelation 1:4-6 (American Standard Version) says, "John to the seven churches that are in Asia. ... Unto him that loveth us, and loosed us from our sins by his blood; and he made us to be a kingdom, to be priests unto his God. ... " Just as surely as Christians are *now* priests—a royal priesthood (I Peter 2:9), the church is *presently* the kingdom of Christ. The same is true of Revelation 5:9, 10. Revelation 11:15 and 12:10 show the triumph of the kingdom of God over the kingdoms of the world because of the blood of the Lamb and the testimony of Christ, pointing back to the cross and the resurrection of Christ, at which time all authority was given to Him in heaven and on earth (Matthew 28:18; Acts 2:33-36). Christ is (present tense) "King of kings and Lord of lords" (Revelation 17:14; 19:16).

QUESTIONS FOR CLASS DISCUSSION

1. Why do dispensational premillennialists believe Christ will come sometime near the beginning of the twenty-first century?
2. Why is Revelation 20 so important to the premillennial theory?
3. Give as many rules as you can (at least three) for the interpretation of the Bible that are especially applicable to Revelation 20.
4. What three things was John writing first century disciples about and where does chapter 20 fit in?
5. What five essentials to the premillennial theory are *not* found in Revelation 20?
6. What is the significance of the "thousand years"?
7. Christ reigns now. How long will He reign?
8. When Jesus comes, what will become of His kingdom?
9. Are you ready?

13

The Hope a Christian Has

I Thessalonians 4:13-17

But I would not have you to be ignorant, brethren, concerning them which are asleep, that ye sorrow not, even as others which have no hope. For if we believe that Jesus died and rose again, even so them also which sleep in Jesus will God bring with him. For this we say unto you by the word of the Lord, that we which are alive and remain unto the coming of the Lord shall not prevent them which are asleep. For the Lord himself shall descend from heaven with a shout, with the voice of the archangel, and with the trump of God: and the dead in Christ shall rise first: then we which are alive and remain shall be caught up together with them in the clouds, to meet the Lord in the air: and so shall we ever be with the Lord.

Much of what we have studied in previous lessons about the rapture, the battle of Armageddon, the antichrist, the thousand years of Revelation 20, and other subjects relating to dispensational premillennialism has been a bit negative as we noted the errors of much evangelical preaching. In this last in the series, we are going to study about some last things in a more positive way.

Christianity is said to have been the fastest growing movement of any kind ever in the history of the world. Jesus introduced the basic principles of His way during His personal visit to our planet, but He kept telling His disciples not to tell anyone about it until He was risen from the dead (Matthew

16:20; 17:9). When the Holy Spirit came on the first Jewish Pentecost day after the resurrection, they began teaching it everywhere they went. Isaiah had prophesied that under the Messianic reign the earth would be full of the knowledge of the Lord, as the waters cover the sea (Isaiah 11:9), and it was so. We are told that by the turn of the first century the disciples of Jesus numbered more than a million.

But it was not without adversity. It was far, far more difficult to be a Christian then than it is now. Persecution was severe. People who embraced the Lord's way were abandoned by their families, rejected by their communities, and persecuted at every turn. Yet there was an unconquerable spirit about the movement that captured the attention and the devotion of hundreds of thousands of Christians everywhere and came to be the mightiest force in the world.

It has been said that it was *hope* more than anything else that gave the early Christians courage, assurance, and joy in the midst of severe persecution and martyrdom. Hope was more than a religious subject they studied and discussed in their assemblies; it was a real, living, and vital force. The abounding joy, indomitable heroism, unquenchable zeal, and conquering faith which characterized their lives were possible only because they looked past their present circumstances and saw the "hope beyond the veil." It was hope that proved to be a sure and steadfast "anchor" for their souls (Hebrews 6:19). They rejoiced in their hope (Romans 12:12).

In these times of uncertainty, unrest, doubt, and fear, the Christian community needs to recapture that blessed hope. So many professed Christians are living in depression, sadness, sorrow, worry, doubt, and fear simply because hope does not burn within as it did in the early disciples.

What was that hope that inspired those people through adversity to victory after victory in the name of King Jesus? Was it the hope of His return to earth to establish His kingdom? No, no, it was not that because, you see, He was already King (I Timothy 1:17) reigning over His kingdom already in existence (Romans 14:17; Colossians 1:13; Revelation 1:5, 9).

Was it the hope of a "rapture" that inspired them? No, that was not it either, that is, not the rapture we are hearing about nowadays. You see, in all the inspired writings, they said nothing about that. Had that been it, they certainly would have said something about it, don't you think? But neither the word *rapture* nor the doctrine is to be found anywhere in the Scriptures.

Was it the hope that He would return the Jews to the land of Palestine, rebuild the temple, restore the animal sacrificial system of the Mosaic Age, and establish a utopian reign from David's throne in Jerusalem for a thousand years? Again, the answer has to be no. Jesus told Pilate that that was not the nature of His kingdom. In John 18:36, He said:

> My kingdom is not of this world: if my kingdom were of this world, then would my servants fight, that I should not be delivered to the Jews: but now is my kingdom not from hence.

Well, what was the hope that inspired and fortified the early disciples of Jesus through all their adversities to victory in Him? Was it a combination of all of these?

The Holy Spirit wrote in Ephesians 4:4-6 that just as there is one God and one Lord and one Spirit and one body of believers and one faith and one baptism, there is *one hope*. What is it? Well, from the passage we read a moment ago, I Thessalonians 4:13-17, it is clear that it was threefold:

> If [or since] we believe that Jesus died and rose again, even so them also which sleep in Jesus will God bring with him. . . . For the Lord himself shall descend from heaven with a shout, with the voice of the archangel, and with the trump of God.

There you have it.

First, they were absolutely certain that our Lord was coming again. And they had reason for such hopes. He had assured them of it Himself. "I go to prepare a place for you," He said. "And if I go and prepare a place for you, I will come again, and receive you unto myself; that where I am, there ye may be also" (John 14:2, 3). What higher authority could a person want for his hope? Many of His parables, such as the one about the ten virgins, were about His return. And at His ascension:

> While they looked stedfastly toward heaven as he went up, behold two men stood by them in white apparel [angels]; which also said . . . This same Jesus, which is taken up from you into heaven, shall so come in like manner as ye have seen him go into heaven (Acts 1:9, 10).

And the Holy Spirit said, "Christ was once offered to bear the sins of many; and unto them that look for him shall he appear the second time without sin unto salvation" (Hebrews 9:28).

So Jesus Himself had promised it, the angels told them He would return, the Holy Spirit confirmed it, they believed it and staked their hopes on it. Because of that hope they counted all things as loss for Him. Jesus had told them no man, not even the angels in heaven, knew the day or the hour of His coming (Matthew 24:36), but many of them expected it to be in their own generation and they lived as though every day would be their last! His coming was so real to them, they lost all interest in material things and some of them just sat down and waited. That necessitated Paul's writing the letters of First and Second Thessalonians.

He said when He comes He will be coming to receive His own to Himself (John 14:3); to be glorified in His saints; to be admired in all them that believe (II Thessalonians 1:10); not to establish the kingdom but to deliver it up to God the Father (I Corinthians 15:23, 24). And that will be the end.

> The heavens shall pass away with a great noise, and the elements shall melt with fervent heat, the earth also and the works that are therein shall be burned up (II Peter 3:10).

Oh yes! It will be a great day of victory for the believer in Christ, but what about the unbeliever? Oh, it will be a sad day, because that passage in II Thessalonians 1:7-10 that promises glory and gladness for the believer says:

> You who are troubled rest with us, when the Lord Jesus shall be revealed from heaven with his mighty angels, in flaming fire taking vengeance on them that know not God, and that obey not the gospel of our Lord Jesus Christ: who shall be punished with everlasting destruction from the presence of the Lord, and from the glory of his power.

Oh say, my friend, you do not want to be among those people! Do you know God through the reconciling ministry of Jesus Christ? Have you obeyed the gospel?

What does he mean by "obey not the gospel"? The basics of the gospel are the death of Jesus for our sins according to the Scriptures, His burial, and His resurrection according to the Scriptures (I Corinthians 15:1-3). Now you cannot obey that, but you can obey the form of that doctrine (Romans 6:16-18) by being baptized into Jesus death, buried with Him in baptism (baptism is immersion), and then raised with Him (Romans 6:3, 4). Have you done that? Will you do that?

Secondly, as an essential part of that hope, the New Testament disciples anxiously looked forward to a resurrection. Death was abroad in the land. Some of their deceased had been martyred and the living knew ere long they, too, would go the way of all the earth. They based their hope of a resurrection of the dead on the resurrection of Jesus. The evidence that Christ had risen from the dead was overwhelming (I Corinthians 15:1-7). It was so convincing that Saul of Tarsus, the great persecutor of Christ, had no alternative but to accept it, preach it, and suffer persecution himself for it. He wrote the Corinthian Christians:

> But now is Christ risen from the dead, and become the firstfruits of them that slept. For since by man came death, by man came also the resurrection of the dead. For as in Adam all die, even so in Christ shall all be made alive. But every man in his own order: Christ the

firstfruits; afterward they that are Christ's at his coming (I Corinthians 15:20-23).

With this kind of hope, they had no fear of death. Though the earthly house of this tabernacle be dissolved, all was not lost. They would have something better, a house not made with hands, eternal in the heavens (II Corinthians 5:1). As in this life they had borne the image of the earthy, so they confidently anticipated bearing the image of the heavenly (I Corinthians 15:49).

Our text says when:

> ... the Lord himself shall descend from heaven with a shout, with the voice of the archangel, and with the trump of God... the dead in Christ shall rise first. *Then we which are alive and remain shall be caught up together with them in the clouds, to meet the Lord in the air: and so shall we ever be with the Lord.*

That is the third element of this threefold hope—heaven. The disciples at Thessalonica very naturally wondered if the faithful disciples who had died would miss out on "that blessed hope, and the glorious appearing of the great God and our Saviour Jesus Christ" (Titus 2:13). Paul wrote them this text so they would not be ignorant (uninformed) and we are blessed by the answer he gave them. He is telling them the living saint will have no advantage over the deceased saint when Jesus comes because:

> The dead in Christ shall rise first [not first before the dead sinner, as the doctrine of the rapture and tribulation has it; but first before the ascension of the living saint]. Then we [the living saints; you see, the sinner is not in this discussion whether living or dead] which are alive and remain shall be caught up in the clouds to meet the Lord in the air: *and so shall we ever be with the Lord* [in heaven] (I Thessalonians 4:16, 17).

Christ will have prepared the place and returned for His own just as He promised, so that where He is, they can be also. He is in heaven.

In his great resurrection chapter, I Corinthians 15, Paul writes of the Christian's victory:

> Behold, I shew you a mystery; we shall not all sleep, but we shall all be changed, in a moment, in the twinkling of an eye, at the last trump: for the trumpet shall sound, and the dead shall be raised incorruptible, and we shall be changed. For this corruptible must put on incorruption, and this mortal must put on immortality. So when this corruptible shall have put on incorruption, and this mortal shall have put on immortality, then shall be brought to pass the saying that is written, Death is swallowed up in victory. O death, where is thy sting? O grave, where is thy victory? The sting of death is sin; and the strength of sin is the law. But thanks be to God, which giveth us the victory through our Lord Jesus Christ. Therefore, my beloved brethren, be ye stedfast, unmoveable, always abounding in the work of the Lord, forasmuch as ye know that your labour is not in vain in the Lord (I Corinthians 15:51-58).

Victory in Jesus! Victory over death and the grave. Heaven!

Well, that is it. That is the blessed hope that inspired the first Christians transforming them into the dynamic force they were—the hope of our Lord's coming again, a general resurrection of all that are in the graves, the good and the bad (John 5:28, 29), and heaven for the believers. This hope inspired the first century Christians to overcome the world and live for Jesus. It brought rejoicing in suffering, comfort and assurance in the hour of bereavement, and joy in being a Christian. The church today must recapture that hope if it is to restore the vigor, vitality, and victory that church enjoyed. It is the only cure for worry and fear and the only remedy for the gross materialism that is smothering the very life out of so many.

I hope you are a Christian and share that hope with all the redeemed today. If not, why not? God bless you. I love you.

QUESTIONS FOR CLASS DISCUSSION

1. Tell the class the evidence you find in the Scriptures of the rapid growth of Christianity in the first century.
2. Describe some of the adversity suffered by the first century church.
3. How do you account for their story of victory and growth?
4. State the threefold hope the Christian has.
5. How can a Christian be certain that Christ will come again?
6. What will He do when He comes? What will He not do? What of those who do not know God and who have not obeyed the gospel?
7. Tell how one obeys the gospel. Have you done it?
8. Why would anyone believe that the bodies of dead people will be raised from the dead (resurrected)?
9. Why do Christians believe in heaven for the saved?
10. How would this hope add greater vigor, vitality, and victory to the twentieth century church?